AF486519

Surrendering Your Self

A Christian Approach to Homestead Heritage
and Other Cults

By:

J.E. Klimek

Dedicated to:
My Step-father, Lee Duncan

who helped while digging through these dark lies

Table of Contents

Introduction: An Unwitnessed Travesty

"'When He [God] talks of their losing their selves, He means only abandoning the clamour of self-will; once they have done that, He really gives them back all their personality, and boasts (I am afraid, sincerely) that when they are wholly His they will be more themselves than ever.'"

-   C.S. Lewis, *The Screwtape Letters*

"…because of false brothers secretly brought in—who slipped in to spy out our freedom that we have in Christ Jesus, so that they might bring us into slavery—to them we did not yield in submission even for a moment, so that the truth of the gospel might be preserved for you."

-   Galatians 2:4-5 (ESV)

Introduction:
An Unwitnessed Travesty

One morning, I was meeting with a friend for a Bible study, and I could tell something was bothering him. I will never forget when he spoke up and asked me, "Have you ever heard of Homestead Heritage?"

It came so out of left field. With how random it was, and his tone, this made me sure it was what he was dwelling on. With nothing else said, my curiosity was piqued. He was not eager to say much until I decided on something on my own.

Later that day, when I had the time to sit down and focus, I did not hesitate to find the website of Homestead Heritage to see what this place was. Finding it was some kind of Christian community, my first concern was to read through their "Beliefs" page to be sure of what I see as the most important part. I thought I would find that was fine, to then take a look at what they did to see why my friend brought it up. However, as I went through the beliefs, little things would not rest well with my stomach.

The first thing to jump out was what they say most quickly of the less common teachings. But not entirely because of the teaching itself. They said they do not believe in the Trinity, yet (only on the website) they still tried to talk as though they do—just another kind of "trinity". And this self-contradiction began to raise my guard.

After going through it, this and multiple other questions, regarding incomplete mentions of the gospel, unclear views of Christ, and odd wordings that sounded like things I'd heard outside of Christianity, made me go back and look more closely.

But one thing in particular raised my suspicions. There is a part of their website that does a Q&A (https://www.homesteadheritage.com /faq/). One question asks about grace through faith alone. The start of this following answer got me:

> The answer to this question depends a great deal on how you define the words "grace," "faith" and "works." In brief, we can say here that we believe, along with Paul that it is "by grace [we] have been saved through faith," and that salvation is "not of works, lest anyone should boast" (Eph. 2:8-9) Yet we also believe along with James that "a man is justified by works and not by faith alone" (James 2:24). We see this seeming contradiction as resolved by recognizing that the Bible speaks of two types of works: works of the flesh that "profit nothing," and works of the Spirit done in obedience to Christ, which are the necessary fruit of genuine saving faith (as verse 10 of the above passage of Ephesians 2 immediately proceeds to describe).

They said the answer was dependent on the definition of those three words, but they never gave a definition of even one of them (I will share their apparent definitions later). I was disturbed to hear them say an explanation was necessary and never give the explanation.

More and more potential issues began showing themselves. A great deal of them were not easily noticed because they were of things I had not looked at before, and I had a lot to learn.

As I journeyed further into their website and other places online, the rest of the week was a dive into the dark, blinding abyss that kept going deeper. With every page, and statement, I read, I grew more concerned I could be reading about a cult (though I constantly tried to convince myself I was exaggerating it).

Though somewhat hesitantly, the next time we got together, I told my friend I took a look at Homestead and explained what worried me. I was relieved when he responded by explaining how he came to the same conclusions I did. Discussing it, we found we were both seeing the same issues, questions, and concerns.

At first, I was just a little curious, but what drove me to look into it further and learn as much as I could was when my friend told me many of our other friends chose to join this "community". This struck hard for many different reasons. Since then, I have looked into multiple cults, but my focus has been on the teachings and history of Homestead Heritage itself.

One of the first things I was told was who Homestead Heritage first pulled in and how he brought more with him. To be honest, before I looked more closely, hearing this confused me why they never said anything to me about it. Deep down, it almost hurt that I would be the one they would not speak to about it. However, looking into it, I realized it happened because almost no one who did or didn't join realized it was a cult, and this made it so they would naturally hesitate to say anything to me. I believe that deep down (consciously or not) they knew I would have an issue with it. They knew me enough to know I would be more cautious than most.

At that point, my sense of being ignored, abandoned, or even betrayed shifted and became a sense of anger where I was ready to do as Jesus and weave my whips to clear out the temple of these liars who deceived my brothers and sisters.

Yet, even with what I found already, the process of learning what and who would need to be revealed took time.

I had to dig deep to find information. Even the first few sources took some time to find. When searching, outside their website, there were some news articles about annual fairs they have, videos done by YouTubers visiting their fairs, and a couple sites on cults that mention it in a long list of cults (but with minimal info). This did not do much to reassure me, nor did it raise my concerns. However, after digging far enough and starting to look back at some of the videos they made on their own YouTube channel, a couple localized news stories about pedophiles and teachings causing child abuse coming from this group caused my concerns to escalate.

After finding out about these stories and looking at them closely enough, I had to begin looking at it with more drive to expose it, but also some fear of what I was getting into.

As I continued looking at their website and watching more of their videos, it was apparent they did not like to say anything simply. They would not speak directly—it was never straight-forward. Seeing this, I realized this webpage did not tell much of what they believed. However, it could easily appear that way if the reader made too many assumptions based on their own beliefs and presuppositions.

I also found some of what one may assume were their "doctrinal statements" were not about their beliefs, but about the faults in others'. Those that were about their beliefs would say a lot with no real explanation. After a great deal of time, and finding next to none of the podcasts, YouTube channels, etc. about cults knew about Homestead Heritage, I decided I would have to take this much further than I originally intended. I had to look at it for myself and share what I found. I needed to keep their lies from staying hidden.

After starting a YouTube channel centered around this topic (Chained Ambassador), I have had many people contacting me. Some are previous members, a few were current members/followers (and I can't help suspecting some of their leaders in a couple cases), and others were members of churches this cult was trying to penetrate.

In some videos, primarily the early ones, there were things I did not understand fully yet, and some previous members were helpful in pointing out what I had right and what I misunderstood.

As I went, I continued receiving more responses via e-mail. Some gave me more information and sources of the cult's teachings. Others were from others being targeted by the cult. Seeing the multiple private e-mails asking for information and/or thanking me for what I put online, because of this need for a warning, I kept digging and sharing everything I could find.

After much reading, viewing, and making videos, I gained a well-rounded view of their teachings and what they really believed. I found that their speaking of Jesus is not really Him as God, despite how they try to make it sound similar, but a man with God in him, and this led their thinking down the road to seeing themselves as the same as Christ. It was finding this and the lack of correction that sealed my concerns and need to spread word.

While exposing this, I found the comments from those defending Homestead Heritage escalated. They would only confirm what I found by trying to judge me for judging and not pointing out anything of their teachings I may have misunderstood. Despite the fact I would constantly ask for explanation in my early videos, they would only rebuke me and never even claim that what I was saying was false. They would only tell me it was wrong for me to expose Homestead Heritage.

Over time, I have grown used to this, and I have reached a point where I no longer have a need for confirmation of my concerns. As this certainty grew, a friend of mine recently suggested I write a book about it and cults in general. Thus, I started this.

I will be going through several things in this book. Understand, it will be focused on Homestead Heritage but also discuss religious cults in general. It may be applicable to some other forms of cults, but those are not my focus, nor have I done as much research into them.

I am doing this because I see a need for those who already have their beliefs to be aware of this. The cults almost always target people who already follow another religion, and Homestead targets Christians in particular. I fear this is because they realize those are the ones who will have their guard down out of an assumption that they could never be convinced to join a cult.

In this book, first, I will be sharing the story of the friends I made who were pulled in, how some of them got drawn into the cult, how I learned about what it was and what it did, and what happened to our relationships in this process. After that, we will go into a bit of what I have read, analyzed, and found makes a cult a cult, how they are formed, and what to watch for. Then, I will go into more of Homestead Heritage's history, focus on the details of what they teach, and give more about how they operate. I will compare it with other cults and point out the contrasts to be aware of. Lastly, I want to go through the best ways I have personally seen to deal with those drawn to a cult, already in a cult, coming out of a cult, and how to keep our guards up against these lies.

My heart has been broken by the stories I have heard and seen of those caught in a cult their friends and family were unaware of. It has been hard to bear how many are getting pulled in because of how their guard is down. I will also share some of the stories of how they got in, out, or their friends were pulled in.

I am doing this in hopes of getting more people on guard. These places sneak in to snatch people from businesses, churches, homes, schools, etc. It is important people are not too trusting or constantly rejecting. We need to accept the truth and reject the lies. We need to learn to make sure it is what *we* believe, not what we are being pushed or forced to believe, no matter who shares it or how they go about sharing it.

Indoctrination can come from the most unexpected places.

[Note: before I get started, I want to make it clear, when telling stories from my contacts, I will not be using real names unless it is someone who has already spoken publicly and shared their position or told me I can. Everyone else, I will replace their names with alternate names. Also, if I share their stories, I will be avoiding many details that won't affect what the story shows to be sure it will not be clear who I am speaking of.]

Chapter 1:

Seeking the Right Community

Most of my life, cults were not a concern. I would hear about them occasionally and found them somewhat fascinating, but I did not have any concerns and thought of them almost as more of an old myth. It made me unprepared for what happened.

Homestead Heritage (what I'll often call HH) never did pull me in, but it has had a major effect on my life by effecting the lives of those around me. It was something I was unused to and not ready for. It was the last thing I was going to consider. If I had given it any consideration, the clues to what was coming were there.

When I was in high school, I was never concerned with having a lot of friends. Everyone would or did say I was an introvert. I would have one or two very close friends, but I would know few others. It was how I lived. I did not go out and join in many activities. I spent most of my time reading.

Being epileptic (and with the condition always escalating), I would be much more limited in what I could do or be a part of than most people. This also made it so it was harder, as well as more awkward, to be in a large group's conversation. I would always sit to the side and only listen in.

This kept me where I was introverted by more than my personality.

But it did not stay that way.

In college I had one of those few close friends you connect with beyond a common friend without even thinking about it. (I will call him Eric here.) Eric and I were always a little different from everyone else. For different reasons (for me, partly due to my condition), we had our own way of thinking that matched to the point we could have hours of conversation and drive anyone else nearby insane with how little they could translate of our way of looking at things. It was something that made us able to talk about those topics we kept hidden deep in our minds so we did not get those strange looks from our friends.

This made him one of the few people I grew close enough to I saw him as more of a brother than just a friend.

About seven years ago, I had Eric come from out of the blue and invite me to a home church at the home of a friend of his. I was hesitant at the time. I normally would have turned it down, but I decided to go because getting to church each week had recently been growing more difficult for me due to how my condition was continuing to escalate, and if there was a friend I knew would understand if I would like this gathering or not, it was him.

While there, I was not sure what to think of it, but after being there for a couple hours, I knew I would want to spend as much time with these people as I could. It was a community I wanted to be a part of. It reminded me of a smaller church I was part of when I was younger, where everyone knew each other well. Even if just for that nostalgia, I could not stop going.

It has been one of the greatest blessings I've had. And what I have learned since has been impactful on what I am doing in studying HH. The irony is there is this potential danger in joining certain fellowships/communities for this very reason I joined the one I did, yet it is also what prepared me.

It becomes risky if that's the only thing, and most, or everything else, goes against one's standards and beliefs. It's about having yourself ready to stand strong on what you believe and to never change it because of pressure from others.

In this new home church, we continued meeting every Sunday. As I got to know them and their teachings/views better, I found they had a different view from me in some of the less central parts of theology. However, this was not an issue to them or myself.

They were not trying to correct me for the way I came from another perspective on the smaller aspects. I did not try to correct them, and they applied no pressure to go along with theirs.

This is what made me consider why they believed what they did, and then why I believed what I did. It was eye-opening for me. As I thought about this, I realized I never had thought through it for myself. The majority of these views and beliefs came from what those around me believed, not from what I found I believed. At the time, I did not realize just how important this was, but I will always be grateful this happened. For all I know, I may have been drawn in by HH if I had not.

After considering this, I began going through the entirety of Scripture for myself to decide what my own views were in many of the debatable topics and some I never considered.

This is something I think more need to do. It is important to be sure it is what you truly believe. Not just because you only learned to claim you do and need to be sure it is your belief, but also because coming to fully believe it and being aware of why you believe it can strengthen your guard. This is what I am now so grateful for.

As I went, I found further confirmation of much of what I believed. However, I also found there were things I always assumed about what the Bible taught, that weren't really there. I found some things made me connect with this gathering even more, and other things kept me certain and on-guard enough to be weary of what came later.

As these gatherings continued, more people joined with us. It kept growing, and we grew closer to each other. We started more Bible studies and prayer times throughout the week.

Eventually, it got to the point we had to start finding multiple homes we could meet in each week. The home we started at was having trouble with so many, so we had to spread.

As this continued, we started to have larger gatherings of those meeting in the multiple homes every month at a place we would rent from another local church. These monthly gatherings were a great time to reconnect and spend time hearing what was happening in the different groups.

However, myself and a friend or two began to have flags raised due to what happened in some of these gatherings and the teachings given during these monthly meetings. We were hesitant to share this at first because we wanted more certainty our concerns were not coming from our own assumptions. We did not want to be causing trouble among the groups for the wrong reason.

We still kept our guard up on what was bothering us and waited to see where it would go. A part of me wishes we hadn't.

We had a friend named Zach who, having studied much theology, was taking care of most of the teaching on these monthly meetings. After a few months of this, we started having the larger meetings more often, and in his teaching for these large gatherings, he began to point too far in one direction. I grew more concerned to notice it was leaning toward legalism with the potential of taking everyone's thinking offtrack.

As he focused more and more on constant confessions of sins

(recent or already confessed), it came to a point where I could not remain silent. Pointing out the issue was hard. People would not see anything wrong with confessing sins, but I could see (partly from past issues) this was getting close to going too far.

I tried approaching a friend, who everyone considered one of the top leaders of our fellowship and also had a good relationship with Zach. Talking with him, I tried to point out my concerns as gently as I could. I wanted to be sure he would see I was trying to raise caution, not to judge. As we talked, he let me know he was confident Zach was not, and would not be, taking things too far, and he saw no issue with where it was at the time to give reason to speak up about it.

Though I was not certain things were good, his confidence did make me try to be more patient with where Zach was going.

After some time, however, I was unable to listen to his teachings any longer. As I tried to say more about it and would start to hint about the issues with it, other friends did not want to consider it a possibility. They would ignore most of what I nudged toward or just assume it had not gone that far yet.

Instead of causing trouble, I decided to sit out on the monthly meetings and made sure to go to the gatherings in the homes where he was not teaching. Zach was going further and further in the direction of making salvation a constant battle of retaining it. It became more and more about what we do and less what He did.

It was as I was close to stepping forward a little more boldly about it, Zach decided to leave California and move up north.

I was pleased to hear this. Not because I wanted to be rid of him, but because I had hope it would be good for him to go up north and have a change of setting. Some of us who had been concerned thought this would give him time away from some of the darker things we often saw with where we lived. It was so much of what he was talking about and seeing in the world that appeared to be having this influence on where his thoughts and teachings were focused.

Our hope was that this would give him time to look at Scripture from a perspective less focused on the subject of sin alone and more focused on looking at the whole picture with his soul more at peace. Too many things seemed to cause him to take his views to one extreme, and we hoped this was a way to be rid of them.

However, this did not work out as we hoped.

A couple years later is when my friend, that I will call Ralph, asked me to look at Homestead Heritage. After I saw the issues, Ralph explained that Zach joined this cult and pulled several others to join it with him.

Hearing this was devastating. At first, I continued doing research in hopes of finding that Ralph and I were mistaken regarding HH's beliefs pointing in a very legalistic and extreme direction of the path Zach's teachings had been beginning to journey down. However, every time I researched it and read their website, articles, books, etc., I found more confirmation we were correct and more issues going in a much darker direction.

The hardest part was seeing how so few knew what this place truly was teaching—including those in it. Many of them I spoke to would often avoid the specifics of their beliefs as though they did not want to know or consider what they were.

After a few red flags, and no one else mentioning HH, I had to do more. I had been put on disability only months before (hard to try and see as only a coincidence now). I found that spending most of my time at home to avoid triggers and unsafe locations for my seizures caused me to use little time doing more than reading and writing at home. I took advantage of this and began sharing what I was studying and concerned by on YouTube. I could feel God was weighing it on my heart. Though I still had to be somewhat cautious, it was not hard to find the time to do the research necessary for this task.

The responses started much more quickly than I anticipated. I found some people were asking me questions, some encouraging me, and others attacking me. Those attacking would normally do it as publicly as they could, while almost everyone thanking me did it in private. But the saddest part was finding how many asking questions e-mailed me privately, because members of their churches were being pulled in by HH.

I found that the reason none heard about it was not just because of how it tricked those outside HH, but also how those who left would be restrained. HH would keep them under pressure to be silent by letting them stay in contact with family and friends, as long as they were not rebuking or exposing HH.

Hearing more about this, I found there were many ways HH found of controlling those who left. It was seeing how they could control and/or hide from those outside their community that motivated what I was doing further—despite what fears and concerns I had making me hesitant at first.

With each video I put up, more people would both come against me and encourage me (intentionally or not), but I also started to have former friends contact me in attempt to defend HH by showing how I misunderstood and was being too judgmental.

This was both the most difficult and the most confirming part of this struggle. They would try to convince me that I needed to visit HH to understand it better. They insisted that I was not in a place where I could say anything against them. I was supposed to understand better what I was talking about by "experiencing" what their community is. (Note: the word "experience" will come up over and over and is one of those they use most consistently.)

When I posed questions about their view of the body of Christ, what is salvation, etc., they would even admit that they did not like the teachings of HH when they first saw it.

Then they would say that when they experienced their worship and met the community, they knew it was the right place. However, they would never say that they now agree with the teaching. If you watch some of what they streamed on YouTube, you will find this said in testimonies. Each time they leave that side of it open-ended. It ends on the note of what a great experience it was, but they never give a solution to the issue of the very teachings of who Jesus is and the gospel HH pushes that they would admit they did not agree with.

This shows the problem that would have kept me from joining our original fellowship when I first visited, if it was there as well. I stayed because of the fellowship, but I would have left if there were teachings that went against my central beliefs. When a place is able to pull people in for this reason, without even noticing or being fully convinced of their beliefs, there is a high chance it is a cult. If it is a religion or other kind of organization, they would not be trying to draw them in to join as members until they knew they believed the same general beliefs.

These groups may pull you in with the community, and then pull (or indirectly force) you into the beliefs, but not just a set of *general* beliefs, but down to the smallest details.

After I spent some time talking with these friends, they would cut ties. Even a friend who has not fully joined into HH, but is following their teaching, has done the same though we are still living near each other. Even when I was telling him we did not have to talk about HH and agree in our opinions of it for us to remain as friends, I could not get past that wall. He went silent and did not contact me after that. He treated it as though I said the opposite and cut ties.

This is the primary reason I can say with such certainty this is beyond just a church of false teachers, but even a cult. My friends have now had to cut ties with me and many of our other friends. Not because of the distance, or carelessness, but because we won't accept HH.

About the time all my uncertainty if HH's teachings were so crooked was gone, I began to find the other friends who had moved and not joined HH were all reconnecting with each other at the same time. I had been unsure who to contact, because I did not know who went there and who did not. As far as I knew, everyone who moved also joined.

Just about everyone who did not move there were all surprised to find that all of us were coming to the same conclusions regarding HH being a cult. As we began reconnecting it brought my hope and drive to another level. Knowing how it tricked our friends motivated us to do more and more to pray for them and warn others.

As we compared notes, contacts, articles, etc. We found all the confirmation we were hoping for and things started to really take off.

I have now contacted multiple podcasts that focus on cults. All but one of them never heard of HH. The exception only recently heard of it and began to put things together. It has been good to see more are becoming aware. The sad side of that is how many heard of it but not what it truly is.

The real identity of HH is well hidden behind a façade often portrayed in a yearly fair. This is what is heard about most often when looking at the articles and news stories about HH. It is the public image they want to display. It is where they show what they do and "how they live" (will discuss this later) to the rest of Waco, Texas.

It was the first thing I learned about when I started looking into Homestead. Seeing so many visiting and hearing about this community, but not truly about what HH is, made me curious how they kept it hidden. That's when the research took another turn.

Looking at their site and others, I found confirmation their community originated in, or near, NYC. Apparently, they were a small church there and the trials and darkness of being deep in the city is what drove them to leave.

This is when I started to understand what was really going on within their teaching.

As I started making connections to different beliefs and denominations in this, I started to discover more of the connections they have outside of Texas. It is putting things together that led to where I am at now.

I have found the difficulty of finding the true past of HH is extreme. Everything they say is misleading in some way. Now, I find myself looking into more and more cults beyond just HH so the comparisons can help in the search.

As I looked for other sources going into the teachings and practices of other cults, I was disturbed to find I could hardly find anyone out there doing it. Most channels and podcasts about cults only looked at their structure and practices, but hardly ever their teachings.

One exception would be Cultish. I have found their videos helpful. However, they rarely discuss cults more people are unaware of. They speak of other religions or massive, well-known cults in most of their videos.

This is why I am now trying to find a way to begin to get more information out there to warn people of what they may be targeted by.

I currently have been on a sort of "hiatus" to slow down on how much I'm looking at HH to look at other cults, and find the sources I need to start exposing more than just HH. This is part of why I decided to write this now. I hope it will be a decent start at getting more awareness out there among those I have found too many cults target the most—Christians.

Chapter 2:

Redefining What is Unique

The question I found I am most often asked, whether out of seeking information or to challenge me, is "What is a cult?" It is one many have tried to answer, and the answer is almost never the same.

It is important to understand this, because it is used more by those defending a cult than those who are trying to oppose a cult. Often, those concerned by a community like this are extremely hesitant to make the accusation (this includes myself). It is something that should be used with caution when talking to them, because it will put them more on guard and deafer to your words. However, it is not something we should avoid using when warning others…and ourselves.

If you are speaking with a cult member and the topic comes up, their definition of a cult will depend on how their cult teaches them. They read, or are told about, some of what is said about cults, but they only consider the features absent in that particular cult.

When talking to, or reading the work of, those who investigate and/or study cults, you will receive a list as their answer, not a definition.

Due to this, the members will take one common feature out of the lists that is easiest to argue is not a part of their cult and use it to try and convince you they must not be a cult.

In the case of Homestead Heritage, they will point to the idea that cults have a single leader above everyone else who started the community. The members will say they do not have this kind of leader so they must not be a cult.

This is very untrue for two reasons.

First, their leader was Blair Adams. Having passed away in 2021, his son, Asahel (or Asi), is now leading HH. He was the one who first led the congregation that moved out to their location. All of HH's books of teaching have credit given to Blair Adams (though sources tell me they are not all entirely by him). And just about everything I've seen them put out since Blair's passing is by Asi. If this is not what makes a single leader, I don't know what they would be willing to call a cult.

Secondly, this is only one potential characteristic of a cult. Too many seem to treat it as though every one of these characteristics must be matched to be defined as one. The reason a list is given is not because they must all be met, but because there are many forms of cults and these are common characteristics.

What I believe causes this to happen is that every cult leader/leadership is all about bringing new beliefs, purpose, methods, structures, etc. to pull people in. It is about being so unique people will be drawn into it by their curiosity or by wanting a different life.

With making things as new as possible, each time the definition can appear to change, yet the similarities are always there. No matter how unique they try to make it, their teachings will also have to have common views to make it more inviting. As it says repeatedly in Ecclesiastes, there's "nothing new under the sun."

The similarities may be there, but which ones are there is always a different combination. When looking at the different standards for identifying cults, there are differences and commonalities in them.

This can depend on what cults may be the focus of those who are creating the list. Looking at these features, here is a more general list of the characteristics I have noticed used most consistently:

- A complete sacrifice to, and following of, the leader or collection of leaders

- Causes the followers to listen without thinking through the teaching

- Separation from other authorities and churches

- Punishment for leaving the group

These may not be enough to help identify every cult, but they are some of the most common features.

There are many others. Some are brought up more often than others, but most of them have a use even if they are not a part of the cult you may be looking into. They can show you more of what the cult's focus and goals are. It lets you know how members may try to defend it indirectly as well as what errors are in the cult. These differences and their uses are why it is good to give all of them consideration.

Looking through many of them to see how many would confirm HH is a cult. I have noticed the differences often depend on what the person/people forming the list believe…what is their religion? One that shows up often if looking at a list or explanation from a Christian source is that cults will add extra teachings that are not part of Scripture. Most religious sources will mention them adding their own theories/beliefs on top of the Bible and/or other documents to fully direct the members in their lives.

Another major aspect of most cults that will come up often while discussing HH is spoken of more often by those not coming from a religious angle. There will be a change of the members. They will have their personality altered. In religions, this can sound like a common teaching. However, in a cult it is more of what Steven Hassan calls a "cult identity". They change the identity to one that is not their own. And HH speaks of it as though any form of individual identity should be removed entirely.

One tool used by many, and I have found useful as well, is a collection of lists Hassan also put together. In *Freedom of Mind*, he gives a list of "Common Characteristics" as well as what is called the BITE model. The BITE model has four different collections of the most common features of how a cult is built—Behavior Control, Information Control, Thought Control, and Emotional Control. It is one of the better tools I've seen for understanding how a cult works. I can say there is little of what Hassan teaches I would not agree with, and even less I would be cautious of. If you want to know more about what cults do and what makes them what they are, this is a good source.

Still, each person trying to define a cult will come up with other features to help cover all the bases.

Yet, when it is a list such as this, those in the cults, those trying to defend the cults, or those in denial of what family/friends are a part of find more reasons to deny the title belongs on that community.

So, how do we really decide if a particular community is a cult?

Most of the religious cults say they teach the Bible. So, let's start by looking at what Scripture says about this kind of topic.

What makes it difficult to get a definition from it is that the word "cult" does not show up, the way we are discussing it, in the Bible. However, what is mentioned multiple times is "false prophet" and/or "false teacher". Continuing to follow HH's way of thinking a cult has that one leader, we can use this to decide how to identify them.

> I am astonished that you are so quickly deserting him who called you in the grace of Christ and are turning to a different gospel— not that there is another one, but there are some who trouble you and want to distort the gospel of Christ. But even if we or an angel from heaven should preach to you a gospel contrary to the one we preached to you, let him be accursed. As we have said before so now I say again: If anyone is preaching to you a gospel contrary to the one you received, let him be accursed.
> -   Galatians 1:6-9 (ESV)

This is one of the first things I noticed looking for Blair Adams's backstory. (I will share this more thoroughly later.) Part of what started his separation from the churches he was a part of was him turning against some of what he was taught.

Many cults will start drawing someone in by claiming to be Christian. However, if one looks into their teaching before convinced by the cult's methods, they will find it is not Christian at all. It is hard to think nothing of it when someone begins trusting a place that tells you it is one thing but teaches you something else…unless you let them tell you as slowly and carefully as it chooses. This is because they will be changing what they teach as they teach.

Teaching so inconsistently is something that is not good in general…as it says in Hebrews:

> Do not be led away by diverse and strange teachings, for it is good for the heart to be strengthened by grace, not by foods, which have not benefited those devoted to them.
> -   Hebrews 13:9 (ESV)

While this passage warns us about strange and various teachings, the other side of this gives another warning. The verse points out how it will not benefit those devoted to it. Part of what communities such as HH are separating themselves to do is to be rid of much of the evil and many of the trials of the outside world. However, there are many examples (primarily those who were sexually abusing children that have been coming out of it) showing how they still do not have this benefit they are pursuing.

Also, this feature is starting to sound more like a cult. Instead of just being false teaching, this is even controlling what you eat and other parts of your life. Cults (whether to the extreme or not) usually try to take a great deal of freedom away from you so they have control.

Colossians says more about this:

> If with Christ you died to the elemental spirits of the world, why, as if you were still alive in the world, do you submit to regulations— "Do not handle, Do not taste, Do not touch" (referring to things that all perish as they are used)—according to human precepts and teachings? These have indeed an appearance of wisdom in promoting self-made religion and asceticism and severity to the body, but they are of no value in stopping the indulgence of the flesh,
> -   Colossians 2:20-23 (ESV)

This makes the definition of false teachings as clear as it could be here— "promoting self-made religion." This shows more clearly what these rules are. When your "church" or "community" starts putting these religious rules on such aspects of your life, that is where the red flags can start popping up.

But one passage in particular would prevent the start of almost every "Christian" cult if the leaders were trying to follow Scripture…

> And we have the prophetic word more fully confirmed, to which you will do well to pay attention as to a lamp shining in a dark place, until the day dawns and the morning star rises in your hearts, knowing this first of all, that no prophecy of Scripture comes from someone's own interpretation.
> -   II Peter 1:19-20 (ESV)

This is what every religious cult has to contradict in order to even start. Going against what is already taught, they either are going to go against Scripture, or they are going to try and create their own interpretation. Whether we say this defines a cult or not does not change the way this will be a characteristic of most cults that are trying to use the Bible.

Looking at these passages, it is showing how any place that tries to add their own rules is not following the Bible, and that any who try to alter the wording or interpretation of Scripture as having a different meaning are not following it.

One thing Blair Adams did constantly is how he used a massive number of translations. At first, I found it peculiar, but it raised my concern the more it happened and the more unique the translations were. I have been unable to find any limit to what he will use. Even though he directly goes against some of the ESV, at other times he will use it.

However, when comparing translations and what he uses, it is clear that he is willing to go to any source he can to find the version that can be interpreted as what he wants it to be.

From this, the cults the Bible is warning of are those with strict religious guidelines and teachings going against or altering what has been taught by the Bible.

If one is looking for a more general definition of what a cult is, I have a potential/occasional solution that came from an unexpected place.

As I've already shown, no one has given the definition of a cult, and they can only give a list of common characteristics. I will say up front that this is the best way to look at it. However, there may be some who want a simpler way of defining it to use as a starting point.

I found a possible answer that I will *not* say is *the* answer. It is only one description that would make it simpler and fits the cults I have looked into.

The answer came from a movie of all places— "The Village". If you have not seen this film, I apologize now for the spoilers.

In this movie you see what looks like a small village of what appear to be pilgrims living in a field surrounded by forests. In this town they have only a few basic rules. These rules are put in place to be sure everyone avoids entering the forest.

The idea is that the forest is full of monsters that will attack them, if they cross the line.

What one learns later is that this story is set in current day. The creatures in the forest are only costumes worn by their leaders occasionally, to scare people away from the forest. These leaders only formed the village to get away from the cities due to trials they'd been through while living there. They created this idea of these creatures to scare the younger people and thereby keep them from finding what is outside their property.

However, they allow the protagonist, who is a blind, young woman, to leave to get some medication for one member who is fatally wounded by another member. They only let her leave because they know she will be unable to see what is outside their property.

When she returns with the medication, the leaders of the group come together and agree to continue the community as it is despite what happened.

When I first considered this movie after beginning to research cults, I found it a little puzzling. Many of the features in the lists are not a part of this community. However, one can certainly claim this is a much more separatist form of cult. This is why I started analyzing this to try finding a simpler definition of what a cult is.

As in "The Village", people join a cult because they think it will remove some or all of the issues and trials they will have to deal with outside the community. It is why those who join are never going to go against the rules keeping them in. They fear what they believe is outside the community.

As time passes and problems arise, they also find things are not as perfect as they are supposed to be, yet, as in the end of "The Village", and I've seen in HH itself, they don't accept how these things show their community does not have the result they were seeking.

It was looking at these commonalities that helped me find a much simpler way of describing what a cult is.

To sum it up, I would generally say a cult is a community that separates its members to some extent from the outside world or other organizations and this community keeps them from leaving via fear.

This is very general, but that is because what that fear is of also varies. It can be a common fear of judgment, a fear of loss, avoiding of isolation, the threat of the dangers of the world, struggles fitting in with those of secular communities, etc. Or it can be as extreme as a phobia put on them individually to gain control beyond just keeping them inside the community. But whatever that fear may be of, I find this method of keeping people in their grasp to be the most common denominator of the cults I have looked into.

This fear is what helps explain so much of what cults do, how they operate, and why they speak the way they do.

When it comes to the religious cults, there is one thing very defining of what they are. They are all about being THE WAY. Not just that the beliefs they teach are the way. It is *them*…they are the way. Unless you are with them you are not going the right direction.

With HH it can seem different, but it is the same with another angle. When you first begin to speak with them, they claim they believe others are saved. However, this is only if these people have not seen HH's teachings. After looking more closely at the teachings, one finds that if someone has seen the teachings, and turned them down, then they're damned. And this leads to where people slowly start to see everyone else as "false" Christians. Then, they will start teaching how those outside HH, and teaching differently, are not saved. It is a long list of teachings leading to this, instead of a single teaching coming out and saying it.

This indirect method of teaching, and way of debating it, leads to something important to remember when trying to use any definition there is of a cult. When people are in a cult, they won't see these false, unbiblical characteristics.

There is always a way to teach it to keep them from seeing it. They are in a mindset where they believe what they have been brainwashed with was their choice. As mentioned, particularly in Homestead, they are made to give up their individualism. They have come to be part of "the Body". This makes it so that when you mention their choice, their choice is the same as the community's, which is the same as the leaders'.

Cults are usually like this. Whether or not it is more or less extreme than HH, depends on the situation, but they will often have the community above the individual in every sense. It is above them in importance, significance, authority, etc. This is why the definition I gave has fear as central.

Fear is the part of it that is about the individual. When you are truly afraid, not just concerned or worried, it is about what could be the effect something or someone will have on you. By making everything that involves your self involve fear, they are making a connection that will make you more evasive of self. I truly mean your self, not yourself. It's not just about involving you, it's about involving your singularity, identity, etc. It is shown clearly within HH's "Confession for Baptism and Communion":

> I further confess that God has convicted me to conform my life
> to the identity of this local church—an identity that is not

conformed to this world, that is not based on self-exaltation, lust and pride…rather that rests on the servant nature of love as manifest in Christ…It is through this local body that I now seek either initial entrance into, or confirmation in, the universal corporate Body of Christ. (p.16)

This is how cults are an elaborate mind game.

Reading through the books of Blair Adams, I could see how he starts with saying what could seem a universal truth. Then, having you in agreement, he throws a curveball to get you to take one of his more twisted teachings by assumption, due to that hint of trust he got from you. Sometimes it is more noticeable than others, but it is always there to lead people to make the wrong assumptions.

That is part of what a cult is. It is a place that wants control of you. It is why it is often one leader. They are the one who wants authority that is not theirs. Whether it be because they have a lust for power or they have the arrogance of assuming they have the answers everyone needs, they play mind games with others to make them follow.

This can bring the question of how cult leaders get their cult started.

Chapter 3:
The Reformation of Deception

Let me say up front, the history of HH is next to impossible to give with certainty. There are many different times HH has talked about its past and/or the past of Blair Adams. Each time, they are incomplete and lacking in useful details. Even many of the former members who were in HH a long time are uncertain of many parts. Different blogs, articles, and videos tell parts hard to fit together or contradicting one another.

Yet, I have been able to sort through it a bit more by the contacts I have who are previous members. For this reason, I will give what I can and let you know how certain I am about each part, but I need to say there is next to nothing I can share with 100% certainty.

The earlier in Blair Adams's life you look, the more inconsistent the information and answers you find will be. What is closest to fully confirmed by much of what he teaches, and what some other pastors say about him (positive or negative), is that he was educated under the teaching of Oneness Pentecostalism.

This also means he started his ministry as a pastor in Oneness Pentecostal churches. However, I have my doubts of how long he did this or if he really was the pastor at times.

Prior to this, HH and some articles talk about him being some kind of high figure in the military, but I have yet to see any details or confirmation of this. Some keep it simple and say he served in the military. Others give the impression of him being some kind of war hero or high-ranking officer.

I do find it a decent possibility he was in the military. However, I see it as extremely unlikely he was in as strong a "position" as is claimed. I have even heard a few things that raise my suspicions he may have been discharged in a way that ended his time in the military on a bad note. This is not something I will say is likely, but there is a decent possibility it is the case.

When looking into what Blair did before he chose to start the "ministry" he had in NYC, there is talk about a great ministry he had of constantly traveling around the country and speaking at many churches without having his own ministry. (Sadly, this has been done by one kind of person multiple times: future cult leaders.) On the other hand, there are other times they will talk about how churches and seminars won't let him be part of it (they have said this as though using it as a derogatory statement of that gathering). However, I see it is likely both of these things were true at different times.

The inconsistency and lack of details in these stories of the time prior to Blair's move to NYC are what makes it difficult to be certain what is true, what is fake, and what is embellished.

When trying to get to what led to the start of Blair's creation of HH, one finds more details in the story just before he chose to head up the east coast. This is where more consistencies and inconsistencies begin to show up.

Looking for this, the story of how Homestead started begins in the seventies.

In the early parts of *Only Two Choices*, Blair explains how he first found his path when dividing a church on the east coast.

This is not the start of HH, but it started the process and shows how things went in the direction they did. As he explains what happens, some things stuck out to me because they are a lack of details. He says he caused a division in the church he was part of about the time things were starting.

This is something I will say with nearly 100% certainty, because it is claimed by Blair and sounds more like something he would not want to spread word of.

The way he speaks of this division is one thing I read and felt confirmed he was a cult leader. It was spoken of during a message he gave to HH. Due partly to this, it is very vague in the details. It gave me impressions of various conclusions, but I'll keep it general.

He said nothing about what he was teaching or saying to cause this division. He also did not go into anything about what he did wrong. In one statement, he says he would start to feel some regret, but God would give him assurance.

This is not something one would brag about, but from his wording, his approach, and what he never spoke of, it was hard to hear it as anything but confidence he did the right thing. (As I'll explain later, this seems to be where their model first started to form.)

When they first started, they came to form ministries in New Jersey and New York. The reason I put these two together is because it is hard to be certain exactly what started first or if they started together. If one goes to HH's website, they give a timeline for this, but other things I have heard tell me differently than what this timeline implies. I am unable to be certain of what exactly the timeline of this was. It is hard to trust, partly because HH's website appears to avoid putting in titles or more precise locations so that it is harder to look for more information.

If you look at the history they give on their website, it is extremely brief. Which is one thing that makes it harder for me to be certain if they are putting it there to show us what happened, or to give us a way of looking at what happened.

I have been given the titles of the "churches" in New Jersey (New Life Fellowship) and in New York (Voice in the Wilderness), but I have also been told there may have been a third. Following the information on their website, the one in New York, probably Voice in the Wilderness (VW), was started in 1973, and New Life Fellowship (NLF) was started in 1976. However, once again, some things I'm told do not follow along with this.

Looking into their history for further confirmation of the dates is difficult. I have found ministries with these titles mentioned in a couple places online, but it appears they have changed immensely from what they started as, or they are different ones that started later. It has made it so I cannot be sure what is really about the ministries Blair started (or was part of).

It appears as though Blair Adams led in VW after moving to New York City. From what I have been told from multiple sources, I logically am led to the conclusion Blair lived in New York while starting VW, but not in the kind of place he claims. He lived in a different part of the city from where VW was located. He also told false stories of hardship in where he was. Some say he was located differently. Others say what I've found more likely—the conditions were not as bad as he claims. This makes it even harder to be certain if there is a third or not.

One thing I have heard, but is never talked about, is a claim of Blair Adams that sounds much like the usual cult leader. He is said to have claimed that those who joined their church would never have to fear death by cancer. It did not take long for this to be hard to keep standing strong…not to mention it was how Blair eventually passed. But this does fit into the usual way of drawing people into a cult at its start.

It also seems the location of VW is what really drove in the direction of moving away from the east coast. If both were in operation when they left, I do not know for sure. But according to their website, they moved to NLF with about 30 members.

They eventually came to the decision to leave the coast when they seemed to begin thinking similarly to the way of the characters in "The Village". Some or all of VW/NLF (about 100) moved to Delta, CO about 1979. There they started what was called "Emmaus Christian Fellowship". This is where the timeline on their website makes itself extremely questionable.

According to that timeline they start in TX the next year. However, there is no detail. It only says, "Church Starts in Texas". There is nothing to say what church or what their connection to it was. I have heard from one of my more trusted sources this was only a branch of HH located in Austin, TX.

However, if this is really any move by them, it may have been a start of a long process. From what I know from my more recent contacts, I have reason to believe this location in Austin was an extremely small "backup" they had (thus why they went to Texas when issues arose). It is something they also do now. It appears they may currently have a great deal of property in other states.

Myself and others have suspicions this is the same kind of backup they appear to have had in Texas while living in Colorado.

Originally, they were doing some of what they now do in Waco, TX there in Colorado. As they started doing more and more with their property, certain things concerned both the neighbors and the city. There were many accusations going both ways. I will say those coming from Emmaus were mostly illogical counterattacks due to the issues the public were noticing with Emmaus.

According to the HH website, they only made the move for more practical reasons. However, given the documents I have seen, I know that there is more to it than that. The relationship they had with the neighbors of Emmaus were tense. They spoke of members of the cult being judgmental and inconsiderate about their property.

The authorities in that part of Colorado were also concerned by the businesses Emmaus was treating as part of their "ministry". After a while of the tension and struggles growing in this as can be seen in documents dated as being written in 1990 (seeing the evidence of these documents is one of the primary reasons I can say with certainty that HH's timeline is not entirely honest; a.k.a. a lie), they left Colorado and moved to Waco, TX.

Here, they remained "Emmaus Christian Fellowship" for a time.

In 1992, a book titled *Churches That Abuse* by Ronald M. Enroth was released. This book was looking at and warning of different churches and potential cults abusing members.

It brought up Emmaus Christian Fellowship at a point where it discussed issues of child abuse. Potentially due to the issues this book pointed out, they changed their title to "Homestead Heritage" to clear-up their reputation.

Looking at their website's timeline, 1994 is when they opened a visitor center. This inclines me to believe it was for the same reason they changed their title around the same time. What was getting out made them more concerned with their reputation in the surrounding areas.

The late 80's to the mid 90's is the timeframe several of those I have spoken with the most left, but the majority of my contacts became a member after this, and is when HH became what it is now.

Going by what I have heard from multiple sources, and what I have read from the books "by" Blair Adams, their theological teachings have changed. Yet, it may not be as noticeable, because what changes I have found to be most substantial came more gradually (reminding me of what I watched happen with the teachings we heard from Zach). These changes are less about teachings being added to what they taught and more about being taught more openly and with more force than they were before.

It appears it was in the 80's and 90's that their current, central rules and teachings were brought to the forefront. Other things have changed since then, but it is mostly within their rules and standards the changes after this had an effect.

In the 2000's and the 2010's, they seemed to be trying to grow more and more on the business side. Though it is somewhat theoretical, I have my high suspicions HH focused most on trying to build a good reputation around their community after their troubles in Colorado, the release of *Churches That Abuse*, and now that they have their new title. Homestead's leadership appears to have modelled what they do in Waco around the prevention of what was happening in Colorado. Now, their reputation is stronger on the surface.

They currently have fairs regularly and do more to promote their businesses. When I was looking up HH, the first results coming up at the time did not seem to be religious at all. At first glance, it appeared to be a traditional community. However, after looking closer it was clear they hid a side of their community from those who did not come to join.

There have been multiple YouTube channels where the channel creators visit different hotels, towns, etc. on vacation to review and rate them. Those I've seen visiting HH often say similar things of not noticing the religious and/or "Christian" side of things while they were there. They did not know what it was until they looked into it more closely after their visit.

This can be a red flag. If they are this community trying to separate from most of society because of the Bible's teachings, wouldn't sharing the truth of the gospel be their priority? How can anyone visit without noticing anything about their beliefs unless they are trying to hide it? It shows their priority is more on their reputation and/or income than on what they claim to be the truth.

Now, HH is continuing to build more on their property and add new businesses. They also have multiple locations across the globe (from what members told me, the most distinct ones are in New Zealand and South Africa). With each of them, I have heard stories from different people about them dividing churches everywhere.

This is their primary method. It is as though everything is based on what Blair Adams did when he first started these "ministries." They will go into churches wherever they are hoping to gain a footing as though they will fully agree with the teachings and support the ministry there, but they will slowly pull those more susceptible into their false teachings.

Multiple contacts came to me out of concern for those in their community who were starting to follow HH and trying to convince others how wonderful the teachings of HH are. Those being pulled in either are ignoring, or don't recognize, those teachings that concern those who contact me. Dividing churches is their goal. This is where HH gets almost all of their followers.

The odd part of this is how few people are in many of these locations. The one in Waco is large compared to most cults, but those in other locations can be as small as a couple families. They seem to use this idea of these being other locations solely so they can look more substantial and trustworthy. From what I have heard, it is as though what "ministry" they have there is nothing but the debris of the destruction they brought when they visited.

It is this way of treating a family or two as a part of their ministry that raises another potential explanation for their claim of a start in Texas beginning in 1980. It may have been nothing more than a family visiting them, or hearing their teachings, and wanting to "join" while staying where they lived in Texas. I still lean toward what I shared earlier, because of the changes from what they were then, but it is another possibility.

As I have more people contact me, it is clear they have not stopped doing things this way. Every time they try to stretch their reach, they do the same thing Blair did originally of dividing a church to pull over what few they can.

There's one thing I have had to say multiple times while talking about cults (especially some of Blair's teachings): "Satan is a fool, but he's not an idiot." This is because he was foolish in turning against God, but he remains more conniving than any other creature. He is the cleverest fool, and cults are among the best evidence of this.

This characteristic is similar to many of the leaders in HH.

When they penetrate these churches, it starts with talking in the usual gospel terms. Everything sounds like what many Christians say. Nothing they say would be accused of being false. But that is what makes their lies so clever.

One challenge Ralph and I gave to our friends who joined HH was asking them what the gospel was, or pointing them toward the video HH did that they call "Two Gospels" and asking if the gospel is in that video. Sadly, they would always claim it fully showed what the gospel is. Ralph and I both were baffled when this first happened. Now, I am starting to understand better why they don't see the problem.

If you ever choose to look at what they claim the gospel to be, before you start, write down the points that are the most important to make sure someone who does not know anything about Christianity understands the gospel. Then begin checking off the list as they mention each point and draw a line through them once they are well explained and explained properly. You may see one or two checks depending on how much you put in your list, but I can be fairly confident in saying there will be not one single line drawn through—and there will be far more missing than checked off. Everything they say can appear true, but the most important truths are missing. Too often it seems people watch for the lies so much they forget to seek the truth as well.

In reality, HH has a strategy similar to what is often done by Seventh Day Adventism. They have these odd definitions of certain words that will change most of what they do mention.

This way of sneaking false teachings into churches comes mostly from HH's uses of ten words: experience, prayer, the gospel, baptism, communion, the Body, faith, grace, forgiveness, and oneness. Though there are more, these 10 are the ones most used in this process of penetrating churches and drawing in new members.

Let's look at these each individually for a general idea of how they can appear to potential members as much different than what they are. Then, we can begin to go through their teaching more fully in the next chapter.

"Experience"

This is a word that could be taken so many ways. That is why they love to use this. It is a simple word you normally would think little of, and they put a lot more into.

To them, it is not just about an experience. It is about THE experience.

If you begin to pose questions about their views or teachings, they will almost always say you should visit HH so that you can experience it. Blair even speaks of it in his books…

> …Christians had lost not only the transforming experience that started their movement, but also the culture in which such an experience could have been planted and then made to thrive and be sustained. (p. 128; *Life Against Death*)

Take note of how this experience is in a certain "culture" and not only that but "planted" in it (this is hinting at what will be discussed a lot later). But as you can see, this is very vague about what he is speaking of with "experience."

It seems you have to experience their community's relationship with what? God? … the Holy Spirit? … or something else? Because you will not what? … be satisfied? … Know what to ask? … Believe? …

Really, they never explain. They only imply one thing: being there to have this experience will cause you to no longer have a reason to pose these questions. Why you won't, what will change, what the experience is, or how it answers the questions they will never explain.

From what those friends, who have visited, told me, these experiences are rather suspicious. Those I trust most tell me they sensed something demonic. After what I have read in Blair's books and heard in their messages, I am unable to deny this must be the case for some and to some extent.

I would have more doubts about this, if they would tell us more about what these experiences are and how the experiences will explain things. However, they are being so vague about it, that I know they are hiding something. If they wanted to convince me of this and it was what they make it out to be, they would not have anything to hide. If they do have something to hide, that raises suspicions about what is being hidden and why it is hidden. That is enough that I cannot trust them.

Trying to decipher what the "experience" is, I have found it appears to be all about "sensing" (in some way) the "love" of their community. This is something I have found sends a chill down my spine. Their use of the word love is different from what most Christians are speaking of when they use it because of how HH messes with the concepts of "conditional" and "unconditional." I will explain this more later, but understand the love they speak of may not be as strong and complete as what you may assume.

They mention this "love" all the time, but what makes them able to identify it as love and as being authentic and Christian is never explained. When you seek an explanation of any concerns you may have, regarding HH, there is always a statement you have to accept fully by faith, even without understanding it. This is a statement given by the members, and thus the leadership, of HH.

That's what the experience is ultimately about, whatever may bring it, it is meant to cause faith in their community.

"Prayer"

Their definition of prayer is rather peculiar. What their definition is depends on the setting. To them, the definition of prayer seems to be based on who is present.

Listening to and watching recordings of various services, I have found that in their publicly online videos and most public services, the prayers are what you would normally suspect when visiting a church service (setting aside some of what is said and the words used).

Looking past this, there are those services recorded but only on audio and not as public. In them the entirety of the congregation joins in as the speaker begins to chant a few lines over and over. However, the congregation is not speaking, but moaning.

Note: for those of you who choose to watch the video of HH about the news reports, the station's recording, HH tries to put in a bad light, is accurate. HH tries to say they did not do it during the service on the video the news station shows. This is true. However, what they don't clarify is if the audio is authentic. I have heard recordings of prayers just like it after Blair's sermons, so I can say the impression the news station tries to portray is accurate.

I have heard the same thing from multiple sources. When these prayers take place, you must follow along with them and be filled with "the Spirit". If not, you are very frowned upon and what is done about it can vary—based somewhat on who it is.

I have been unable to hear recordings of what I have been told they do by a couple former members. They say it is much more extreme—at least in some locations. There seem to be much more "private" meetings where it is not known about as publicly and even recordings are prevented. I have been told that in these, the moaning gets to a point where it is so loud some have their ears in pain, and at times people almost get violent in appearing to lose control.

Again, everyone needs to be filled by "the Spirit" during this. It is the forcing of this on people that raises the real red flag for me.

Why?

When you are being made to groan as loud as you can either in order to be filled with "the Spirit" or to appear as though you are, your attention is certainly not focused on anything you are praying for, nor on anything you may hear from Him. And especially, you will not put any thought and analysis into anything the preacher/speaker may have said or what is being prayed for by anyone leading the prayers.

That is a tool of brainwashing.

"The Gospel"

This is the slyest part of all their lies. Because this is the most important part of Christianity.

How they hide this I will give more detail about with the topic under "faith". Here, I want to start off by explaining what the gospel is really about to them.

HH has a document they call their "Confession for Baptism and

Communion" that is/was required to be signed by new members before they were baptized and made part of the community. It is a massive document that I had to do 10 videos, over 30 minutes each, to cover what it is teaching even though I did as little apologetics as possible, and new members are required to fully embrace everything in this document. I will mention it multiple times, because another and much longer book could be written, if I chose to go through everything it teaches.

After talking about how the old sinful nature is washed away by the saving blood of Jesus, it says this:

> This latter occurs as the believer continues to walk in the light (I John 1:5-7) in an *ongoing* washing that comes by Christ's Word (Eph. 5:25-27) and through His Body. (p. 49)

This is very deceptive in many ways. First, the first passage is not saying what they are saying. They take it and reverse the order and then ignore verses 8-10 with what they teach.

> This is the message which we have heard from Him and declare to you, that God is light and in Him is no darkness at all. If we say that we have fellowship with Him, and walk in darkness, we lie and do not practice the truth. But if we walk in the light as He is in the light, we have fellowship with one another, and the blood of Jesus Christ His Son cleanses us from all sin.
> If we say that we have no sin, we deceive ourselves, and the truth is not in us. If we confess our sins, He is faithful and just to forgive us our sins and to cleanse us from all unrighteousness. If we say that we have not sinned, we make Him a liar, and His word is not in us.
> -   1 John 1:5-10

Secondly, the second passage I would say is being used in a misleading manner. It speaks of "washing that comes by Christ's Word," but it says nothing about its need to be an "ongoing" process for the salvation of Christ's blood.

However, despite whether or not these passages fit here, what leaps out at me is not the references given, but the part that has no reference. His "Body" (which I will talk about more later) refers to the church (or from their views, HH). So, they claim it is the church or your own joining with, and growth by, their church that washes away your sin. Going by this, HH is teaching salvation is not done fully by Him, nor is it done by your works and His. It is done by your works, His, and your relationship with the "Body."

Later the same document says, at the end of this very section—once it has brainwashed enough,

> This means that Christ is not so much our *re*presentational substitute as our presentational substitute, a substitute whose sacrificial life and presence we must enter… (p. 55)

Thus, it is ultimately not by His power. His power is only there as an example of what we are to do. by us following what He was showing we must do. Given what was said earlier, they claim the true gospel is not about forgiveness by Christ paying the price, but true forgiveness by following his example through the "Body"—HH.

If you look at that last quote, you can see how carefully they worded it to make it so it can still sound like the gospel. They want anyone who is reading this to be a part of "the Body" to look at this carelessly and assume it does not really mean what it actually says. However, for it to truly be read as the gospel, you have to take "representational" (when something/someone is standing in the place of) and "presentational" (demonstrational) as the exact same meaning or use potential confusion to flip them. Or you have to do as I fear too many do— take it as meaning what you already believe because figuring out exactly what it is saying is too complicated…if you want it to be correct.

There is one place Blair shows what they truly believe the gospel is in *Is the Church Christ On Earth?*…

> If, then, in your mind and heart, you destroy God's means of forgiveness in the expression of "Christ coming in the flesh" of His church (as we've earlier established), then where will you find the sacrificial life of Christ on earth, the life through which you can first enter Christ's atoning sacrifice and then begin partaking of God's long-suffering and forgiveness, which Peter says is our salvation (2 Pet. 3:15)? (p. 65)

If you want to look at II Peter 3:15, you will probably be rolling your eyes, as I did, at how this has nothing to support what he says. It is here he shows they see their community as what the gospel is reliant upon. Not simply from "Christ's atoning sacrifice", but by first finding "the sacrificial life of Christ on earth" by "His church". They are your salvation according to this gospel.

This is what they are indoctrinating with.

"Baptism"

When looking at most of HH's documents and books, baptism can seem to have the usual definition…until you read the "Confession for Baptism and Communion".

This document is so long, as I mentioned and showed before, and almost every topic starts off saying what most Christians would agree with but ending in something way off track, if not flat-out heresy, that alters what was said previously. It is this long, drawn-out way of making you think you agree with them and then giving you a lie under that façade that can make this document so effective. And yet, this is supposed to be solely for baptism and communion?!

The first question that needs to be asked, and is answered only if you are seeking (not just asking for) the answer, is why all of these teachings need to be followed for something that is such an early step in being a Christian as baptism?

Oddly, this is the one part of this that should not be as difficult to notice. Yet, you have to be alert from the first word and not read too quickly at the start. It is how it starts off in the first sentence in the introduction called "Important Instructions". The part many might assume carries little weight as far as what is to be agreed to. However, everything of what baptism is can no longer be what they are speaking of because it says,

> You have received this material because of your request to be baptized into, to transfer the context of your allegiance to or to receive communion *within this fellowship*. (emphasis added)

This is something I will bring up and discuss much more closely in the next chapter because the reason for this is very deep under the surface. However, what you can notice by this before understanding their beliefs entirely is that, to them, baptism and communion are not about your salvation and relationship with Jesus Christ. Instead, they make them all about your membership and relationship with them (HH).

With so much under the surface to explain later, this clearly shows how they use ignorance to help brainwash.

"Communion"

For HH, there is little difference between Baptism and Communion. As Jesus says, it is supposed to be "in remembrance" of Him. However, they make it more as "in remembrance" of the member's original "baptism"—dedication to HH.

When both of these things are symbolic of what He did, and the price He paid, they are replacing the gospel with what they are doing and what price you will pay (to them).

"The Body"

To dig into what this is, there is one concept to keep in mind. He is the head and we are the body (Colossians 1:18; Ephesians 5:23). HH rarely mentions these passages, but right after the few times they do they go on to teach teachings that throw it out.

If you didn't notice, when they mention the body in their documents, instead of putting "the body" they put "the Body".

They see the Body as Christ Himself. As Blair says in *Is the Church Christ on Earth?*

> But once Jesus' sacrifice and resurrection is complete and the church is born, everything dramatically and radically shifts—it shifts from Jesus speaking through the individual who was miraculously born in Bethlehem and who died at Golgotha, to the *corporate* Christ through whom the Head now speaks. This is because the church is now called the very Body of the same Christ who was God manifest in the flesh, the kingdom *directly* ruled by God. (p. 9-10)

According to Blair's teachings, the Church is Christ. Not that it represents Him. Not Christ guides/controls the church. Not that we carry His testimony. They truly call themselves Christ.

Within this framework, who is the head?

The leadership of HH.

Thus, they indirectly teach that now the leadership of HH are the ones who have truly become Jesus Christ. This is how the people follow them and following their teachings can be required so often in the "Confession for Baptism and Communion" to be treated as though equal to His Word.

I recently met up with a friend who has been visiting HH and listening to many of their teachings. He joined in on a Bible study unexpectedly. At one point, speaking of himself, he claimed he could say, "I Am".

This is how they are able to make the act of baptism and communion all about your dedication and unification with HH.

This is how their teachings are so misleading!

"Faith"

This is where their definitions get to be the most frustrating for me personally, partly because this is where they lie the most bluntly but still complicate it so much that they can be sure few understand fully what they are saying and they are not ready to try to understand it.

If you look at what they define it as in a blog on their website (https://blog.homesteadheritage.com/what-is-the-gospel/), you can find the best explanation of what this word means to them. But, again, they try to make it sound good at first, but watch what is implied in this…

> Being led by the Spirit to do the Father's will flows from an active faith and devotion—a vital relationship with God. In short, you can't please the Father without faith, and you can't obey Him unless it comes from a heart of love. He's not requiring the minimal demands of the law any more. He's requiring so much more. He's requiring our hearts, our minds, our will, your whole self. That is called faith.

Note: it says, "you can't please the Father without faith, and you can't obey Him unless it comes from a heart of love." There is an implication here that could easily be missed. Normally, when making a statement such as this you would be saying, "you can't have A without B, and you can't have B without C." Read it again asking what is really being said there with regards to this line of reasoning.

It says you "can't please the Father without faith" and "you can't obey Him" without "a heart of love." The first part of this treats faith as B. The second part puts obeying Him as B. When looking at it this way, it can be seen it was accidentally showing how they see faith and obedience as the same thing.

If you doubt this, look at where it said, "He's requiring so much more." When put this way, it means they are not necessarily saying you don't have to follow rules anymore. They are really saying you need to do that and more. This is how they hide their view of the gospel.

But, setting these two things aside, the big thing is one thing added here that many may miss. It sounds good to say, "He is requiring our hearts, our minds, our will, your whole self." Notice two things: first, they go from saying "our" to saying "your", and second, previously we talked about how they want you to be rid of your self. (There is a reason it says "your whole self," not "all of yourself") When this is said, they do not mean what we mean when we say something similar to it.

By requiring "ours", they are focusing on the Body. By saying "your…" they focus on the self. As we discussed before, they use "your" only when it is something they think you should be rid of. There would be no need for a change in the pronouns, if you meant this in the way most Christians would mean it; you would just say, "He is requiring your heart, your mind, your will, your whole self." (Though that last part could still be corrected depending on what you mean by it.)

Ultimately this is claiming faith is all about giving up your self to be in the Body. Everything they call "ours" is what you need—to be part of the Body, you need their heart, mind, and will once rid of your self. When they talk about this obedience to Him, they are really thinking the obedience to the Body. Following what we've already seen about how they use these words, it means that here, near the end of this document all about "faith", they are claiming that faith is about your dedication, obedience, and giving everything, but not just to Him but also to HH.

The simplest way to put it is that they see obedience to their teachings as being faith instead of faith causing obedience to Him. They take the meaning of "faith" and treat it as synonymous with "faithful". They flip the cause and effect.

This is why they are able to hide what they are teaching about the gospel. With this word being all about your obedience to them, everything of the gospel is made to no longer lead in the direction of the gospel. It is all about obeying their standards to be saved and believing in the "Body" instead of believing in the true Christ.

Very dark and complicated indoctrination.

"Grace"

This is the most convoluted word they use. Of everything I could tell HH was misusing, this is the one I found most difficult to find their definition of, and there is still more to what they are trying to do with it. When reading what they write, or hearing their messages, I sometimes respond to them using "grace" the way I would respond to teenage girls using "like".

However, there are times they are being clever how they use it, and it is good to at least have a general idea of how they would use it within their framework.

For them it is not ultimately about receiving what you do not deserve. It is not about grace being this gift. Instead, they try to put grace where there is none. They talk about it as though God is gracious by giving the opportunity to earn something. It's almost like saying "he stopped you," when what you meant was "he let you stop."

As you can tell, this is nothing more than them wanting to use a word used all the time in Scripture that does not fit into their theology. So, instead of treating grace as something granted or given, they talk about it as though it is more of the potential that something could happen than the fulfillment of that potential. (Which causes multiple paradoxes in their teaching.)

This is a façade or an excuse.

"Forgiveness"

This is very similar to the way they use "grace".

The difference is that they use it in a different place instead of just changing the meaning. They don't bring up forgiveness much when it comes to the gospel. When they do, it has to do with forgiveness of one another. This use can seem good at first, but there is still something they change about the meaning.

Their "forgiveness" is not permanent.

One friend had to leave HH after he noticed what was wrong. (I'll call him David.)

David had been with them for some time and been following their guidelines of confessing everything to them. Particularly one time when he left randomly, because David needed some time away from HH. After confessing what he did, they made him spend time away from his family—where they put him to reflect on it.

After some time, David decided he was leaving.

After he left, they sent him a letter in which they used everything he confessed previously to them to try and bring shame upon him and pull him back into their community.

This is not forgiveness. It is definitely not God's form or way of giving forgiveness.

If it was only about how they forgive each other, I would not be so concerned. However, what makes this of such significance is how it makes the leadership's forgiveness, instead of God's, what matters.

"Oneness"

I listed this last for multiple reasons. The primary reason is that how often they use it is dependent somewhat on who they are speaking to.

One teaching they have going against many in Christianity that they will be quicker to bring up is oneness, but this word has a much different use to them.

Oneness is often used for the teaching that there is no Trinity. This is something HH teaches, though differently. However, when they use the word "oneness" they are speaking more often of their community when they use it.

This is one I have trouble determining if they are intentionally changing the word or not. If so, they are using it to confuse people who don't know what they teach.

To them, oneness is about the unity of the Body because they have died to themselves. They are now part of the Body and have a oneness with each other.

This can seem like an odd teaching that is not too extreme, but there are times it even implies it is not just them. It is them and God. It is a subtler way of bringing up what they believe the Body is and how it works.

This can confuse those coming from the same background as Blair. It is often used in a similar way to the other words discussed, but it will only have the same affect on those who come from those teachings.

This is how HH can claim to "honestly" share their beliefs while hiding what they really teach.

It is what made me constantly doubt myself at first. It was receiving their baptismal agreement that made everything clear enough for me to be certain they were deceiving people in this manner.

This is why I have been trying to put what they really teach into terms people will see properly without learning this other language.

So, keep these meanings in mind as you see the other quotes I will give from HH in the next chapter. It is by remembering they are practically speaking another language that you can come to understand what is being said in many of these statements.

Chapter 4:

Teaching What is Never Said

This chapter is a difficult one to put into order. There are too many things to discuss.

I want to do two things in this chapter. I want give fuller explanations of what HH teaches. I will also start comparing this to what it seems many religious cults teach similar to HH and what parts of HH's theology are rarer.

Most topics with regard to their beliefs should be discussed here. However, if you want more details about certain things, you may want to check the videos on my YouTube channel (Chained Ambassador) where I go through some of their documents and give a detailed explanation of their baptismal agreement. (However, keep in mind that the earliest videos on the channel were before I received this document to have a clearer view on their teachings.)

Though they claim on their website to be closest to anabaptists, there are similarities to many religions in the teachings and practices of HH. There being too many to go through, a relatively simple list would be Christianity, Jehovah's Witnesses, Mormons, Judaism, New Age, and, as mentioned, Seventh Day Adventists.

The reason I make a comparison to Mormons and JW's is because of their view of Jesus Christ—the most important part of Christianity. True Christianity is seeing Jesus as not just the Son of God but God. Some take this view of the Trinity while others follow the Oneness teachings. In Oneness, most have a modalist view—often saying God takes different forms at different times.

The latter is what HH can appear to be at first glance. However, once one looks more closely at what is said, one will find a mix of what is found when you look closely enough at Mormon and JW teachings.

It is hard, at first, to consider this because both Mormonism and HH will constantly push how Jesus is the Son of God. But when you watch more carefully what is said by both, particularly in their private practices, you will find they do not believe He is *the* God.

In the case of HH, it is most noticeable in *Is the Church Christ on Earth?* In this book, Blair says this:

> So it was because Jesus called Himself "the *Son* of God" that they said He was making Himself God…to claim to be "the *Son* of God" was, to the Jews, to "make yourself God," a truth that Jesus did not deny…In other words, He is totally and completely obedient to and dependent on the direct will of the Father—He has no other mode of operation for His life except doing God's will. He is one with the Father because He's completely dead to everything else. (p. 7-8)

As always, Blair begins by trying to make you think he is agreeing with most of Christianity's belief of Christ being the Son of God. However, where a Christian would say, "...and He is God," Blair says "He is...obedient... He has no other mode of operation for His life except doing God's will. He is one with the Father..." not because He is God, but "...because He's completely dead to everything else."

Or, as he says in *Life Against Death*:

> Somehow, in other words, people had to at last come together in a oneness with God like that which Jesus made manifest in His own life. (p. 132)

You may have noticed in the earlier quote I gave, from *Is the Church Christ on Earth?* Blair said, "...Jesus speaking through the individual who was miraculously born in Bethlehem..." This shows they do not see the man Jesus as truly being Jesus. They try to make it sound like they do, but they teach it differently so they can make their Body out to be the exact same as what Jesus *was*.

Blair stated this more plainly in one message where he said, "...there is no rest, except in Jesus. And there is no Jesus, except His Body as He expresses that body on earth."

This shows similarity with the Mormons and JW's. But particularly Mormons in both how they view Christ as well as in how they try to make it so we can eventually be equal to Him. This teaching is the central issue.

As carefully as they can, HH makes the church (a.k.a. the

Body…a.k.a. HH members) Christ himself.

As we already saw it also said in *Is the Church Christ On Earth?*

> …you destroy God's means of forgiveness in expression of "Christ coming in the flesh" of His church…you find the sacrificial life of Christ on earth, the life through which you can first enter Christ's atoning sacrifice… (p. 65)

They make the need of Christ's departure for the Spirit to come out to be due to how the Body is now Christ. Until Jesus left, that would not happen, because God is one. (Yet, there is so much irony in how they contradict their own reasoning by making Him so many more than three.)

Blair held to this teaching so strongly, that he would flat-out misquote Scripture. As mentioned, this can be by using different translations, however, he will occasionally go as far as to put it into his own words and still put quotations on it.

There is one passage I've seen Blair twist more often than any other…

> …till we all come to the unity of the faith and of the knowledge of the Son of God, to a perfect man, to the measure of the stature of the fullness of Christ…
> -   Ephesians 4:13 (NKJV)
> [Note: when quoting Scriptures they use in their texts, I will usually use the NKJV because that is what I have been told, by former members, HH normally uses.]

What he quotes it as saying (multiple times) is far different…

You see, we are the ones upon whom the end of the age has

come, the ones destined to receive this great promise, the promise of the resurrection Spirit, the promise that reconstitutes us as sons of God and then leads us on in triumphal procession into "the full measure of the stature of Christ, a perfect man." Yes, this is the promise that carries us into the child of the promise, who is Christ—born of God. (p. 38; *False Faith versus Saving Faith*)

The way the passage is quoted here is used by Blair in other places (and still put in quotations). Here it may not give the reference, but he does in others. What he never gives is what translation is being used. And I have gone through every translation I can find. I have even searched for portions of this quote online to find any translation or any person who may have quoted it this way before. However, I have never found it used this way anywhere. What makes this even more disturbing is that the closest I have seen a translation come to saying this is in the NWT (the version of the JW's)...

...until we all attain to the oneness in faith and in the accurate knowledge of the Son of God to a full-grown man, to the measure of the stature that belongs to the fullness of the Christ.

When I found this, I had a chill when I saw how the JW's chose to word the first part of this verse—it is way too much like a translation I could imagine Blair would prefer.

When considering this, it can be seen Blair is rewording it to make it about us having His stature instead of the fullness. This passage I've seen him misquote most is used to put us on the same level as Christ.

This is why the one teaching HH will push the earliest in their teachings is their denial of the Trinity.

On their website, they try to claim they believe in an "economic trinity". This is misleading. There is nowhere else I have seen them use this term. It is only put where their "beliefs" are the most public.

What this really is, is closer to being a different form of modalism. Yet, it is only similar and starts in a similar place. Modalism sticks to most teachings of Christianity and just tries to explain what is in the Bible without accepting the Trinity. HH, on the other hand, doesn't truly see it as God taking different forms, but entering Jesus and then entering us. It could almost be taken as a form of "multitasking".

Now, I would normally move on to the next topic, but there is something they say in their baptismal agreement I need to confront. But this forces me to clarify something first.

I strongly disagree with the Oneness teaching. I see it leading in a dangerous direction if one starts looking at the correlating passages logically. However, I also believe there are many who have that belief who are still Christians, because they do not always come to the conclusions it can lead to. For this reason, I will stand against the teaching of the Oneness Pentecostals, but I will not say everyone who follows it is not a Christian.

I clarify this because HH goes the other direction in their *Confession for Baptism and Communion* during a portion where they are pushing the teaching of there being not only One but also that no one believes in the Trinity:

> I sincerely confess that the Spirit of the Lord has revealed to me, in keeping with the millennia-old heart of Biblical Judaism, that a divided or tritheistic God has no place in Biblical Christianity, which makes emphatic and essential the non-negotiable belief in the one God of Judaism as incarnated in Jesus… (p. 8)

The document often pushes this idea that belief in the Trinity ("divided") is the same as tritheism. It is by this statement they are claiming I am not a Christian, and that those friends I had to watch join HH were not Christians until they accepted the teachings of HH.

This goes back to how they often talk as though they are not against Christians following some other teachings, however this, and other parts of this document, shows they are misleading in this because they do not believe those who believe in the Trinity are Christians.

It is out of these buried teachings about who God is and how they view Him that many of the other issues grow.

One issue already mentioned in passing that is significant for other reasons than just theological ones is that they teach God's love is conditional.

What they teach with this is distorted well (I will go into this further in later chapters). Ultimately, they claim that God's love is conditional based on if you are falling into sin or following "Him". It is given this characteristic to fit in better, not with their teaching, but with how they structure their community.

Unconditional love can be a major issue for many cults. If they follow this teaching (or claim to), they will be flat out lying because of how they structure their community and view the outside world.

HH has a clever way of convincing people of a conditional love, so it will give the leadership the freedom to bring God's judgment as they so choose.

This is a part of it I find hard to spend time on for personal reasons. This is a topic I discussed most with friends who started following the teachings of HH.

What I did go over roughly, but not fully explain earlier was what aspects of Zach's teachings bothered me before he left. In hindsight, I see this as the very reason he was drawn into HH and why they accepted him as they did to now have him in a position of leadership and even teaching in their conferences.

What I explained generally was how I was being bothered by Zach's teachings because he started treating it as though battling against our sins was all that mattered. Sadly, from what I could see, it seemed to be because of his struggles with his own shame.

I can understand why many loved his teaching. He knew a lot and, when he chose to, was great at comparing different passages and showing the connections between the Old and New Testaments to show how the symbolism and prophecy of the Old Testament did so much to point toward the New. However, these teachings started being taught less and less often.

What bothered me was that I felt like he was still battling inside himself with sins he had repented of when he joined our home churches. It got to me because I knew the feeling and had struggled with it myself. Because he could not seem to get rid of his guilt, he acted as though everyone else must be going through the same struggle as him.

As this was happening, myself and a couple others were worried our friends were like the frog in the urban legend of one in a pot of heated water and letting it reach that boiling point.

Initially, it was not something to speak up against. The topic of our sins is a good issue to speak on. It is a topic that should come up from time to time, but he slowly started making it ALL the time. There was not necessarily falsehood in it when he started doing this, but the water had only been poured into the pot.

Over time, the heating got it to a point where you had to repent constantly for your sin. Eventually, there were hints of pain from the heat of its implications of the inclusion of those sins you repented of in previous repentances. As this teaching bubbled to the point of repenting constantly to retain your salvation, there was another side I started to notice when it was too late.

Heading down that path in his teachings caused Zach to begin looking down on, not many, nor most, but all churches. He was seeing any connection with the world as though it would mean you put it above God—given his teachings, putting it above "the church" is closer to what he would really mean. This extreme sense of separation due to a conditional love is what put it in place.

What I realized after the fact was how this put him in a place where part of the move out of California was not only to get to a place far from the cities but one where they could also have a community more separate from not just the way of the world but the way of all other communities. As HH already shows, it is also what leads down this path he eventually took.

It was in this new community that HH visited Zach and started drawing him, and those following him, in.

When this started, they turned the knob up full and the pot boiled over to the point many of us were horrified, but some were enticed by the smell of the meal.

The teachings of HH push toward the salvation by works. They say salvation by works and faith, but you have to remember what they are really saying—salvation by works and faithfulness. This was what Zach had been slowly moving closer to with each message he gave. When they offered this, he dove in.

Following this train of thought fit the other side of what Zach was pursuing. It led to where the best way to be certain of your salvation was to get away from anything that could not only trap you in sin, but even make your thoughts unfaithful in any sense. The only way they could see this done where they could have a feeling of certainty was to separate away from everything else to the extreme.

It is the similarity to Seventh Day Adventism of the redefining of salvation with such subtilty that I can say truly pulled my brothers and sisters in. It was going the direction they were tempted to go and had all warning signs taken down. I had my doubts about these warning signs before I learned what HH taught, but I can now quote two statements of Blair Adams that seal it.

In *False Faith versus Saving Faith* Blair speaks of what is involved in salvation as "partial faith" and insists we need a more complete faith (faithfulness/works). One of his most disturbing, and convoluted, statements comes when he explains this.

> On the other hand, works that the Bible portrays as 'dead' and evil basically constitute simply doing our own will. This verdict is not challenged or even mitigated by the fact that we may claim it is God's will. Works may even be merely believing human theological constructs and creeds about God and salvation, while at the same time standing outside any genuine relationship of power with God that would walk us through the appropriate interpretation of truth—in other words…we merely get baptized, and then we "believe" that *that* takes care of everything; or we merely mentally assent to a certain set of theological facts or to a creedal statement of faith, or we merely "profess" Christ and then the humanly constructed "belief" in the saved-by-Christ-*idea* takes care of it all as far as salvation is concerned—but there is certainly no "living" "by the power of God" in any of this, as Paul described saving faith. Rather, any or all of these constitute "works"—human mental constructs that we believe in more than we trust in and obey God Himself… (p.10)

I must confess, I was ready to throw the book across the room in rage when I read this. Following this logically, the teaching of being saved by faith and not by works is "'dead' and evil." Yet, here it not only messes with what faith is, it even starts flipping the meaning of "works" to be faith. Every time I read this, I want to tell myself I must be misunderstanding him, but every time, I go read it again with the previous and latter paragraphs only to find extra confirmation that yes, he is saying works is faith, faith is works and, if you believe differently, your beliefs are dead and evil.

Another thing mentioned twice in this that I want to point out is where it speaks of His "power". Both times it is mentioned when Blair starts speaking of what it is that we need instead of just this "partial faith". When looking at the first place it is brought up one can see it is this "power" "that would walk us through the appropriate interpretation of truth." In other words, we need this special "power" to understand what salvation really is. He is speaking of the "experience".

However, it does not end there. After showing what is this partial faith, he later says this:

> It [partial faith] submits as little as possible, as if cutting a deal with God to purchase salvation from hell as cheaply as possible, thus making a mockery of the great sacrifice of Calvary. (p. 32)

The hypocrisy of this statement enrages me. He wants to make us feel like we are treating salvation as cheap by not expecting we have to pay a price. Yet, he is treating Christ's death as cheap by claiming it is not enough to pay the price on its own.

With a teacher telling us that our deeds are stronger and of greater worth than the life of Jesus Christ Himself, how can we call him anything but a heretic?!

In his other book, *Only Two Choices*, Blair pushed it there as well…

> [Jesus] came, in John's words, to "destroy the works of satan." But this would only occur *within* a called-out people who would receive the same power of the Spirit that gave birth to Christ and then raised Him from the dead… (p. 31)

He says it could only occur in people with the power of the Spirit. He treats it as though Christ cannot complete what he came to do on His own. He is saying it is not until everything the Spirit did in Christ is done in us that it is complete.

Apparently, Blair believed Jesus was mistaken when He said, "It is finished."

It is also these teachings and this way of following them that leads in a direction where you are inclined to give more honor to your leaders than true Christianity would. It is what has to be there in every cult for it to work.

It was this shift in honor that brings so many to follow this, whether it be out of inner pride, or because one puts a brother in too high a position.

Their practices of baptism and communion are what take this to that place where you are holding their leadership above everyone else.

As I mentioned in passing before, *the Confession for Baptism and Communion* is the document that finalized some of my concerns and suspicions. It being the start of their membership in HH, this detailed explanation of these teachings makes certain they agree with all of them, but also, there are many places where they are careful with their wording and description to keep the unbiblical aspects of them from sticking out.

This is what makes it hard to go through this document. You have to pay close attention. And you have to pay the same close attention to *all* of it. Because they only want you to pay attention to what they are telling you to profess, not what they are causing you to believe.

At the end of the introduction it says,

> IF YOU HAVE DOUBTS, UNCERTAINTIES OR QUESTIONS ABOUT ANY OF THESE POINTS, OR ANY ISSUES CONTAINED IN THESE CONFESSIONAL STATEMENTS, THEN CIRCLE THE STATEMENT AND NOTE YOUR UNCERTAINTY OR CONCERN. TAKE THEM BEFORE THE LORD IN EARNEST PRAYER UNTIL YOU PRAY THROUGH TO A CONVICTION. WE CAN ALSO DISCUSS YOUR QUESTION AND POSSIBLY GIVE YOU LITERATURE TO READ ON THE SUBJECT, UNTIL YOUR DOUBTS OR CONCERNS ARE ANSWERED AND SETTLED.

It is insisting that everything in the document must be agreed upon, but it says to "pray through to a conviction." They try to keep you from just deciding not to join, they push for you to be fully convicted on your decision. They don't say, "pray about it before making a decision." Instead, they want you to push to the point of this "conviction". If you feel led to turn it down, it will not feel like what is implied by "conviction". By definition, it is only when you admit to faults in your previous beliefs and views that you feel convicted. They point in this direction to indirectly cause you to force yourself to agree to it.

It also tells you that if you need confirmation they will "discuss your question and possibly give you literature" (note, not Scripture) to remove your doubts. They are not telling you to decide if you agree or not. They are telling you to push yourself to agree with them. It shows the final authority in this is not being treated as Scripture, but as their leadership, and possibly more…

I have heard from one contact I will call Martin how he was talking to a friend in HH and the question of what was his favorite book came up. Martin told him it was one of Charles Dickens's novels. His friend got upset. When I was hearing this, I thought Martin was going to tell me his friend was upset he did not name a book of the Bible. Instead, his friend was upset that he did not name one of Blair Adams's books. Martin has told me this happens many times where they appear to hold Blair's books as high or higher than Scripture by how often they use his books, carry them around, quote them, etc.

They push this need to follow HH's leadership again, where they also hide a lot by putting many questionable/incorrect things within portions of a biblical statement.

In this document they have you sign, it says near the end,

> I realize that my signature to all aspects of the foregoing confessions does not mean that I will never unintentionally sin or fail, but that I will never fall into habitual sin, hide *any* sin, break covenant or rebel against the authority I have confessed is sent by God. (p. 135)

The last part of this emphasizes the authority they believe the leaders of the Body have been given by God. (Note: "any" was emphasized in the original document—I did not add it.) It is this document that not only makes sure you agree with their teachings but that you will put the leadership of HH on that pedestal to be the head of the church—in other words, the head of the Body—thus, following what they teach, the head of Christ.

Also, as I have shared earlier, their treatment of one stumbling and the requirement of a communion to "rejoin" at such times shows the rest of the list is not truly what they practice.

The baptism and communion of the members is not about just one's membership in HH. That is the most prominent part at first, but as one goes further into the document, there is more added to it. Thus, what it said here at the end is about one's dedication to the leadership of HH and *their* teachings.

But it must be the leaders of HH specifically because of what was said much earlier on.

> ...I can now confess in all integrity that God Himself has absolutely convicted me that only a suppression of the truth in unrighteousness (Rom. 1:18), a suppression so deep as to amount to apostasy and therefore bringing wrath, could ever make me turn my back on this truth and then join myself to any even nominally Christian group that has not received this revelation from God. (p. 14-15; *Confession for Baptism and Communion*)

This counteracts everything I have heard them say about not being against other Christians. But not only that, it also makes turning from HH the same as turning against God. Therefore, it will bring His wrath. This is then used later to make it so they will feel a need to come to agreement with the document, even if they disagree.

That's how it works—fear.

They have this need of being in charge of not just your life, but what you believe.

> Every scripture we turn to seems to put forgiveness, salvation, deliverance, healing, miracles, and all else pertaining to what God would do for us in the context of an ordered fellowship of brothers humbled in the flesh and walking in the light of the community of believers that live by the Spirit, walking in the light of the Body where brother is loving brother. So, now, even "passing from death to Life" hangs on whether we love our brothers… (p. 37-38; *Is the Church Christ on Earth?*)

That is what a religious cult is all about. In churches, the members never agree with everyone on every topic. Yet, they stay together because they have their priorities in particular places. Cults force absolute agreement on everything—your beliefs, your work, your daily routine, what you eat, what you wear, even "your" preferences. This is a need to be in absolute agreement, but not with each other. It must be with the leadership.

One Earnest Hemingway quote says, "There is nothing noble in being superior to your fellow man; true nobility is being superior to your former self." I have never been a fan of Hemingway, but whether intentionally or not, this quote has a more Christian point than every cult and is something most cult members need to learn.

There is a point where HH takes its similarity to Mormonism and goes in this direction making them the cult they are. Where HH starts most clearly going in a different direction from Mormons is in how they use these teachings about becoming a part of Christ in their baptismal agreement. To HH it is not about the individual being Christ or a god, but about how each individual needed to "die to self" to become part of the Body.

As they put their twist on salvation, one thing Jesus called salvation is something HH tries to avoid or distort what they can—being reborn.

By what is said in parts of Scripture (John 3:3; I Peter 1:23), we need to be rid of ourselves to be born again. HH is against this—they alter that terminology. They want us to die to our selves, to become a part of the Body and never have a new self.

> ...He declared those strange revolutionary and almost universally misunderstood words, "You *must* be born again." Contrary to today's clichéd usage, His wasn't a creedal statement but an imperative for the root transformation of every human existence, a change of outlook and world view so complete that the transformed individual would give himself wholly to become part of the Christlike community... (p. 168; *Life Against Death*)

They treat it as though, because you are full of sin, you have to be part of the Body instead of yourself and be rid of your self.

If truly going by Scripture, we are supposed to be made anew. We are supposed to be transformed. What they do is incomplete. Putting a violent dog in a cage with a muzzle is preventing some injuries, but it is not training the dog. You cannot change yourself, if you are rid of your self.

In the baptismal agreement the new member must agree to this:

> To accomplish this, I confess my need to also share completely in this local church's identity, which God has shown me is one with His, and His own chosen identity for me. (p.17)

Note how this is showing they see it as no longer being their identity, but the identity of the Body itself and it "is one with His." This is trying to make the members of HH God indirectly.

What is almost ironic is where this can lead. To be one with those of the Body and thus God, it leads their thinking in a direction making it more understandable how they could take in a great deal of teachings with a more New Age way of thinking.

When I first started looking at HH, I was curious and concerned. But the first thing I read that truly disturbed me was the name that was a correlation between multiple quotes on videos and sites and the subtitle of one of Blair's books—*Life Against Death: The Struggle for Sustainable Communities; From Gandhi to Today.*

This is what first made me concerned if there was any kind of connection (indirect or direct) between New Age or Hinduism and HH. Looking at what they do and what they push most in their daily lives and teachings, I have found that ultimately, the New Age ways of thinking are the kind of model HH encourages most.

The connections with New Age that are easiest to notice may also go unnoticed because they are found in so many religions and views with so many different perspectives. The two clearest are "oneness" and loss of self. Yet, HH holds to them in a way that will appear to be as Christian as possible and keep them from going in a direction that would be easier to connect with New Age teachings. This is something they have done constantly.

I must, for a moment go on what may seem a tangent to set the stage for what I want to get into.

Another name Blair brings up in *Life Against Death* is Simone Weil. In case you do not recognize the name, she was a French woman from the first half of the 20th century. Her beliefs were, in my opinion, fairly chaotic (thus unsurprising Blair uses them). Somewhat similar to Gandhi, she had a wide range of religions her beliefs appeared to come from. This is why it is not so surprising to find the two of them are brought up in this book.

This is going to be a long quote to share from *Life Against Death*, but please read it carefully, because there are multiple things I will need to talk about in this…

Now, what does she [Simone Weil] mean by all that—"Unless

you possess a radiance of which the energy . . . is equal to [or we might even say, that "exceeds"] that [energy] contained in your muscles," you cannot be nonviolent and therefore, by implication, cannot die happy? She means, I believe, that without this visceral power of preternatural love, whose great energy carries us beyond lust, beyond our own selfish interests, beyond wrongful enjoyment, a love that must at least equal, if not exceed and transcend, the driving forces of our physical being, then we will simply give way to the bodily mechanisms of self-preservation, including the wrong kind of enjoyments that ultimately lead to the wrong kind of death, either of self or of others. In short, if lust, which is rooted in the pleasure principle and therefore seated in selfish and self-centered interests, is not replaced by love as the driving force of our lives, a love that is rooted in the interest of the other rather than self-interest, then there is nothing to take us outside of the agony of our death and to transcend it in the ecstasy of standing outside ourselves in the pure joy of loving the Other. (p. 157-158)

This may be confusing. If so…you are thinking clearly. If you did not notice, this is only three sentences. This is something Blair does often. He rambles on and on, but not randomly. Instead, he does it to try and weaken your guard and get these ideas you would normally be weary of to slip past your reasoning and plant them in your brain where you won't notice it.

I have to admit, I almost did let it slip by. If it wasn't for his capitalization of "Other", it may have gone unnoticed in my reading. However, when you stop and look at what the sentences ultimately say, it is much simpler.

First, consider how he says, "She means, I believe…" What she said was fairly short with a very New Age sound to it. When he says this, he is almost taking credit while having the easy way out. What he says is not what she said, but it is what he wants to think she means. If he was trying to reword it to be understandable, he would have simplified her quotation so it could have said it clearly enough. Instead, he goes and tries rewording it in a way that will be lengthy enough to get the ideas, and his own, across without having that New Age wording there to make it something others may be uneasy with.

Notice, Blair starts off that last sentence saying, "In short," (oh the irony that he thinks this following sentence is short), in other words, "to explain."

One reason I quote this whole section is to show you how one could easily read this and, if they are disturbed by the statement at the end, be made to assume it is above them. However, I came to see what was being said despite being confused my first time through. It was reading more carefully for what he was trying to say, instead of being distracted by the side notes, that showed me how this was trying to make a false teaching seem brilliant.

To make it simpler to read, the last sentence is saying this: "if lust is not replaced by love…there is nothing to take us outside…outside ourselves in the pure joy of loving the Other." Considering this with what has been said in HH's baptismal agreement, it is saying we will not know real love until we are rid of our selves and part of the Body. This is where one side of New Age is the most deeply hidden and having the greatest impact on their teachings.

When seeing how he wrote this, the similarities they have with

New Age are what they deny the connection of most. It is these clearer connections that thus do the least to show the link. It is by less direct teachings the real connection can be seen and is how they get into so many churches without being exposed.

Sadly, I can't blame anyone for not seeing this. I had to choose not to settle with not being sure what he was saying. I had to push myself to make sure I fully understood.

What drove me to this point of looking into what was not understood also came from *Life Against Death*. It talks about Gandhi in ways that first brought me to a point where I had no room left to deny something was wrong with their teaching.

> So again, in regard to the core dynamics of what Gandhi represented—nonviolence and resistance to industrial culture—it makes no more sense to see this as the result of only New Age influences or only Hinduism than it does to see diverse people or movements, such as Christ, Menno Simons, Einstein, G.K. Chesterton, Zionists, Martin Luther King Jr., the Catholic Land Movement or the Southern Agrarians as either "New Age" or Hindu. (p. 122)

This quote can be disturbing in so many ways. All the figures it lists along Christ's makes me uneasy how they seem to be treated as on the same level.

When you can say it about Christ, why do you need to list anyone else? (Note: Blair lists Him first and then puts this long list of names between there and the real statement.) But what gets to me is how this is putting what Gandhi represents as being just as New Age as Christ.

His wording tries to give him a way out by saying we would be treating Jesus as "New Age" or Hindu. While with Gandhi, he added the word "only". However, if one tries using this way out, it only makes his whole statement void. He even says, shortly before this,

> …Gandhi rejected Blavatsky's more occult notions, and while he did draw heavily on her favorable view of Hinduism and vegetarianism, nonetheless, he kept his own counsel … (p. 113)

Even here he has to admit Gandhi used it heavily. This is why he had to use the world "only" to cover his bases. It was this part that made me start to watch this book's teachings more carefully.

It was disturbing to read through the many ways Blair sought to excuse or explain Gandhi's errors. He would constantly push how Gandhi's reputation for being New Age was only because of something he studied while younger. He would imply Gandhi abandoned it later, but he never gave anything as far as quotes by Gandhi. It felt like the majority of the book was all about convincing the reader Gandhi was a godly man even if he didn't know it. This led to Blair lying to us and himself more and more bluntly as he went.

At another point in the book, Blair takes a lot of time making a distinction between current day New Age and previous New Age. Blair treads it so carefully it is too drawn out to quote. It is clearly something he feels a need to be as cautious and precise as possible with his wording to describe. He tries to push the idea that what Gandhi taught and followed was completely different from what New Age is today.

Blair tries to talk as though these two forms of New Age have no similarities. Considering this, reading that quote again has everything thrown on its head with no explanation. Which New Age is he speaking of in this quote? Was the later mention of New Age the same New Age as the first mention? When he tries to create such an extreme distinction between the two, this other quote means nothing. However, either way, this ultimately shows he does have to admit Gandhi did follow New Age. Even if it was of a different kind, it makes it clear he is searching for a way to make people believe he's not New Age, but he can't.

But this would not be a big deal if he only admired a certain teaching of Gandhi, but there is more that was said not long after the first quote… "It is also a call for great courage, such as that which Gandhi unfailingly displayed." (p. 159) It paints an image of Gandhi where he is a perfect example…yet, Blair did not say something like that about Christ. If you read *Life Against Death*, you will find the majority of this book is there to try and convince you Gandhi was a good role model of what Christianity should be. As you may see in these quotes, it also keeps Christ from standing out as THE role model.

When I saw this, I received confirmation my concern, that I was seeing some New Age teaching, was well placed.

In a document, called "Questions Visitors Ask" that I received from previous members of HH, there is a massively long list of answers for their members to give. In this Q&A document, a portion of it is about their farming and use of the land.

Though this disturbed me that they would have to explain to their members how to answer simple questions about the society they live in, the reason I feel it is crucial to bring up is because it is within this that I saw more of the New Age thinking sneaking in.

The statement that seemed to come out of nowhere and made my denial go silent once again was at the end of this:

> It is true that we might *temporarily* get better yields by "shooting up" the land, like an athlete or race horse pumped full of steroids or amphetamines in order to win a race. Yet in the long run such methods deplete the life of the soil and add sometimes dangerous, disease-causing chemicals to food (as well as degrading and demeaning the value of what you "shoot up"). So we choose instead the rhythms and music of the returning way. (p. 12)

This last sentence made me feel, at first, like someone was speaking in tongues and I was unable to translate.

Yet, despite all the other sources pointing to this link, the most ironic and obvious is in a website that would be expected to have nothing to do with HH: Mother Nature News (to see the article, its web address is listed in my bibliography). It mentions how HH would never be expected to be a "Christian" organization, and they compliment it for how it is so concerned with the preservation of nature. But, the most striking statement for me was when it said,

> We work with Homestead Heritage through the MOTHER EARTH NEWS FAIRS, where they promote The Ploughshare Institute for Sustainable Culture.

I have never heard of HH connecting with any other organization or ministry. Much of what they say would lead me to assume HH would avoid doing so. Hearing they did was surprising, and hearing they did it with this organization was disturbing.

When it came to the teachings of HH, this underlying New Age perspective of nature snuck in many tiny places, but the most prominent inserts were in *Coming Into Orbit*.

I will go into some more of this book later, but here I have to say there is a lot of misuse of Scripture in this book. I won't go into all the details here. I have given more discussions of this book online, but here I'll keep it within reason.

Looking at the passages in context always changes the meaning Blair gives to them. It is a short read, so if you are curious how they get people to take in New Age, this is one way to know.

But, to give a single example, here is a part that stuck out to me:

> Let us take time here to show in some detail just how crucial these orbits and this order is to the entire universe. Paul wrote that "since the *creation of the world*. [God's] *invisible attributes are clearly seen, being understood by the things that are made*, even His eternal power and Godhead" (Rom. 1:20). (p. 13-14)

Here is the passage it quotes with more context:

> For the wrath of God is revealed from heaven against all ungodliness and unrighteousness of men, who suppress the truth in unrighteousness, because what may be known of God is manifest in them, for God has shown it to them. For since the creation of the world, His invisible attributes are clearly seen, being understood by the things that are made, even His eternal power and Godhead, so that they are without excuse, because,

although they knew God, they did not glorify Him as God nor were thankful but became futile in their thoughts, and their foolish hearts were darkened. Professing to be wise, they became fools, and changed the glory of the incorruptible God into an image made like corruptible man—and birds and four-footed animals and creeping things.
- 	Romans 1:18-23 (NKJV)

Blair started the quote where he did, and ended it at the end of that verse as well, so that it could feel like an encouragement to follow these teachings in a way similar to New Age teachings. By removing verses 18 and 19, it keeps the reader from understanding this is about what it shows against ungodliness, not what it shows about what godliness is. It's about how nature shows His power, not how it has been given His power as implied by what Blair said before the passage.

It can be hard to notice this side of their beliefs at first. New Age itself keeps sneaking in on different Christians, because of how good it is at hiding itself. So, when it comes into a cult like HH, even where it comes up, it is well hidden and not discussed as much. The New Age aspects are there more in the application from a New Age perspective. Thus, many who visit HH, or hear some of the sermons, may not catch on to this influence though it seems more prominent than others.

When they take on these teachings similar to New Age, JW's, and Mormonism while also pushing how so many Christians are not "true" Christians, it creates the drive to go along with some of the more cultic aspects of their teachings and community. This is why they need an "experience" to pull people in deep enough.

I already explained some of how they take advantage of one's experience. What I have not explained much of yet is how they try to push this view.

When I first heard them talking about this, they would keep saying, "You will recognize them by their fruits." They would basically say, "…look at how loving they are…look at the blessings they bring… you have to 'experience' it to be able to judge it…"

I have to admit it kept me silent. I was scared. This passage was something that would bother me every time I thought about it. I did not want to go against when Scripture says, "You will recognize them by their fruits." But it always seemed to be an issue because of how loving some people can seem to be without believing in Christ.

Hearing this argument from them was the first time I found they were silencing me. I am so grateful God had them push me to the point where I finally looked at it again.

When I finally took the time to look at what this passage said, I realized I had always heard that phrase in a loose way. Aside from some sermons I may have been distracted during, I never heard it used in relation to the context of the passage.

It is a similar use of Scripture to the one we just looked at. The first passage mentioning it says this:

> Beware of false prophets, who come to you in sheep's clothing but inwardly are ravenous wolves. You will recognize them by their fruits. Are grapes gathered from thornbushes, or figs from thistles? So, every healthy tree bears good fruit, but the diseased

tree bears bad fruit. A healthy tree cannot bear bad fruit, nor can a diseased tree bear good fruit. Every tree that does not bear good fruit is cut down and thrown into the fire. Thus you will recognize them by their fruits.
-    Matthew 7:15-20 (ESV)

This passage is used by members of HH to explain why their "experience" while visiting changed their perspective despite the issues. The problem of only using, "You will recognize them by their fruits," comes from two places.

First of all, those who use this passage never explain how they know who the "them" is. So, they ignore how it starts. Secondly, they give their own view of what the fruit is without showing you how Scripture describes it.

Reading this I was stunned. When I paid closer attention, I noticed it is talking about the fruit being from trees. I was used to spending more time considering the analogy used when talking about the vine and its branches. Neither of those were talked about here. This was a different analogy. So, what was this talking about?

To define "them" there is little that needs to be read. This started off talking about the false prophets. Thus, this passage is giving a way of identifying them, not a way of identifying who is of the Lord. Also, there is another place where this same image and statement is made and explained further. It shows what this "fruit" really represents in this particular analogy:

Either make the tree good and its fruit good, or make the tree bad and its fruit bad, for the tree is known by its fruit. You brood of

vipers! How can you speak good, when you are evil? For out of the abundance of the heart the mouth speaks. The good person out of his good treasure brings forth good, and the evil person out of his evil treasure brings forth evil. I tell you, on the day of judgment people will give account for every careless word they speak, for by your words you will be justified, and by your words you will be condemned.
- Matthew 12:33-37 (ESV)

Again, it speaks of how, "the tree is known by its fruit." The difference is that here it also goes into the type of fruit it is speaking of. This is not about showing love or having an "experience". It is about what you say. In this passage Jesus is speaking to pharisees. Thus, this is talking about what they teach. It is about the very thing HH is trying to use it as an excuse for.

When it speaks of the fruit of the Spirit, it talks about knowing His true followers by their deeds and the love in them. When it speaks of this fruit on the tree, it is speaking of knowing the frauds by their teachings. They are both about identifying the believers and those who are not followers, but they logically would be identified by different fruit. The love proves who really follows. The false teachings prove who is a wolf in sheep's clothing. When one has love, it does not prove they are an authentic Christian if they teach falsely. When one lacks His love, it does not prove they are an opponent.

No analogy in and of itself would be considered a crucial part of theology, but making it seen accurately becomes so when it is being used as an excuse for being careless about what you believe and teach.

My anger always rises when thinking about this. They are trying to make you treat it as though the teachings are not so important. Yet, when you choose to join, they force you to read a 140-page document and sign each part of it to make sure you follow these teachings they claim are not so important.

It is the inconsistencies and hypocrisy I noticed that first made me more on-guard and suspicious of each of their teachings. And I heard these inconsistencies from my friends who had warned of things like this only a few months prior to joining HH.

It is also in this inconsistency that their beliefs can become difficult to find because they do not always fit together.

One of the more difficult parts to piece together is what they see their goal as. They often talk about evangelism on their webpages talking about their beliefs, as well as in certain books Blair wrote. However, as described earlier, no one not connected to HH can really tell you what this community believes. Evangelism is clearly not on their priority list. So, what else would their goal be?

They do often talk as though they are all about the "unity" of the "Body" and bringing it together to build the "New Jerusalem". However, everything they do to try and grow goes to dividing churches instead of unifying. So, unity is clearly not what they are trying to bring.

They sometimes make it look as though they are about going into a more "natural" way of living and avoiding the world. However, from almost every source who left more recently, I have been told how a great deal of that is a façade they put on while visitors are nearby. So, they clearly aren't so dedicated to that cause.

What is their purpose?

Each of these, and none of them.

Their goal is (as mentioned in passing) being what they call the "New Jerusalem."

The evangelism is not to reach out to the world. It is to bring in the Christians and change their theology. The unity is not about making all believers able to work together as a body. It is about pulling who they can into *their* control to be part of *their* Body. The use of the "natural" means is not to make sure they are not using what is mechanical. It is to make everyone see them as outside the influence of the world and at one with nature.

This last one is the more confusing and disturbing for me. The question I often asked was, "Why would they care what people think of them in regards to this topic?"

It took me a while before I realized what was going on. It was what I'll call their "indirect separatism".

Making those who join assume they would leave all of technology behind makes it so they will give up many of the things that could lead to them learning of things about HH the leadership does not want them to know, or hearing teachings outside their model that could show them the issues.

When considering this, I realized they were partly correct when they would claim they were not "separatists". I call them indirect separatists because it is not as much about staying away from everyone else as it is staying away from what things could "lead them astray."

It is why they can contact friends and family, *until* they start to go against HH.

I can't say for sure how accurate it is, but I heard some talk about different, newer members feeling "proud" that they have come to a place where they avoid all books outside HH's. Anything that could hinder them from blindly accepting these teachings is shunned and forbidden—another feature in most cults.

During one live stream I had on YouTube (which I received strong negative feedback for), I showed a photo of Blair's tombstone, which one of his quotes was put on. It said,

> We dream because we love and love because we are loved—because we are our Father's children, children who know no better, who have chosen to know nothing else.

This is more befitting than I would have expected… "Children who know no better," is a quote showing how they approve of what is considered a bad thing by most. This follows one of the more consistent characteristics we mentioned of cults. They do not want you to think for yourself. (Again…dedication to avoiding your self.) You need to follow their teachings and know nothing beyond that.

This is where a comparison is most often made to the Amish. Of all the things I can compare them to, it is the one I find the most insignificant, yet I have heard the most people use it. It is ironic because those supporting HH will speak of the Amish being so much stricter, yet many who have left or only visited HH will say it is much worse than the ways of the Amish.

I will rarely make this kind of comparison, because the Amish communities vary immensely and rarely act in the manner of a cult (though some do). Also, the Amish are more authentic in their lifestyle and avoidance of modern tools, based on what I've seen of them.

With HH, its similarities to the Amish are too often nothing but an act. Their concern is not in holding to these rules. Their concern is holding to the ones they rarely speak of as openly. The ones that are seen are only to be seen.

The stories I have been told of what they do when people break the rules are dark. I cannot tell with much certainty what is real, what is exaggerated, or what is misunderstood. The majority of the time, whether the "punishment" comes physically or mentally depends more on the age of those who broke their rules. Both ways are rather extreme, but I cannot say they are as extreme as some of the worst cults. However, there is a consistency in the stories that tells me HH does go too far.

This is where things get most disturbing for me personally, because they don't always stop when someone leaves. It is a mind game they continue playing. When something goes wrong for those who leave, they have, at times, been contacted by HH and told it was God's punishment on them for turning from the Body.

This is when I started to notice where their teachings would come out from under the surface. It is always in the rebuke of others that they are as open as they could be. It is also where they slip up more often than I suspect they intended. This is what I want to focus on in the next chapter.

They keep so much of their teachings and beliefs within a façade, but when you start watching what they do and how they act with regards to those around them, you start to see what the teachings and beliefs are causing in their followers.

Chapter 5:

Controlling a Kingdom

One very good friend who visited HH told me a story that paints a great image of what HH does in relationship to the outside world. I will refer to her as Mary.

Mary visited HH not long after I learned about it. At the time, I did not know she was going to go to visit HH, or even that she knew about it. She heard about it from some of those friends we lost to the cult, and her and her husband visited to see it for themselves. Her stories went anywhere from unsettling to terrifying.

What Mary shared that struck me hardest was what would seem the least upsetting of the stories.

They were brought into one of the homes of the families of HH. The gathering had them share a bit of their story. After and before, everyone stood around eating some food that was prepared. Other than that, they did nothing. And I truly mean they did *nothing*.

For a while they just stood around the room being silent. Mary found it awkward, but those of the cult acted as though it was normal. It remained uneasy with Mary unsure what she was supposed to do until everyone started leaving.

Later, a friend who already had joined HH approached Mary and appeared to be pleased with what happened. When Mary asked questions due to her confusion, they told her everyone remained silent because they do not speak unless it is the Spirit speaking through them.

When I heard this, I felt like I was just shown what HH truly was.

If they are part of the Body, the Body is made of all filled with the Spirit, and those who speak must be speaking by the Spirit, then who the majority of the followers of HH are hearing from are those at the top. It is what you see anytime you are in contact with them. They only speak if they are rehearsing what they have been given to say by those above them in HH (thus why they would create a document for "Questions Visitors Ask"). They are all standing in a silent room with nothing to do until instructed on what to do or say.

This is what the teachings are there for. They are not truly creating a community for the sake of their beliefs. They are making beliefs and teachings that fit into the model of life they want to follow. And for the leadership, it creates this little world they have complete control of. These places are often led by those seeking what Satan sought, if not more.

They want the authority that is God's. They want to create their own world where everyone follows them. Where everyone worships them. Yet, unlike what God created, they want there to be no choice so they have even more control.

This is the definition of evil.

To be honest, I would not be that against HH if it was what most see it as (a different form of Amish community). I would still have my concerns, but those issues would not necessarily be due to the model itself. What makes me so against it is how it forces you to follow that very way of thinking and makes it so you are following another god.

You have to start off wanting this quiet place to live. Then you have to listen to what they say because of the authority they have. Later, you will not speak because you must be rid of your self. Then, you only speak when it is from the "Spirit" (their guidance). It is why I am so heartbroken to be able to say, "They are my friends, but I don't know those in HH." My friends are not the ones I'm seeing or hearing when I get to speak with them.

Being so controlled removed all control.

It creates paradoxes similar to some of those that show up within a lot of New Age. One of the most significant ones comes from that issue of identity. It is seen most plainly in one part of *Coming into Orbit*…

> Unless you find the cure of a humility that says, "You know I could be wrong in this," then you can be sure that you're not feeling the Holy Ghost. All you're feeling is the intensity of your own flesh and its insistent stubbornness and pride, clinging to your own opinion and ideas. There's no humility through which God can speak to you and through you. You don't have the honor it takes to know God and to follow Him, and you're going to

someday fly out of orbit in a truly frightening way. (p. 39)

Blair seems to contradict everything else he teaches in this. He seems to teach humility is good, pride is needed, yet humility is causing issues, though honoring your self will make *you* able. New Age has the same contradictions of finding that balance with nature and everything else, yet it being all about you becoming your own "god".

These teachings come out when Blair is talking about the members' tasks and positions. Just as it is with New Age being more about practices than beliefs. This is why these things will carry such contradictions.

The reason Blair teaches like this is because he needs you to be humble under him, but you have to have some "honor" so you can do what he gives you to do.

At another point, he teaches,

> And if your choice is to come into conformity to His will and within His orbit, think about what you're doing to the whole universe. (p. 60-61)

When it says "what you're doing…" it goes against so much of the teachings. He does not teach this because it is what they truly believe theologically. In the other statement it pushed the necessity of humility. Here it is pushing it is something you need to do. Not only that. It is also making what you do as though it will change the universe. Yet, notice how this goes against his own teaching by saying "what *you*'re doing…"

He changes his teachings and approach once he is discussing

how they are to go about doing what they do in their everyday life. It is because of how he is leading them in what they do. By convincing them they have such endless influence while they are serving him, it reassures him they will be doing everything they can for him.

And yet, he also says, shortly before this,

> We don't want to see you just serving yourself to us in pride—we want you serving Christ to us, and we want you to offer yourself up as a living sacrifice so that there's less and less of you and more and more of Christ. (p. 56-57)

In the same book, it says,

> We just don't know the bounds of our limitations, of our orbit. We don't know the boundaries of our abode, of our place, so we don't find God. He's right there, but you don't find Him because you can't recognize the limits of your place. You weren't brought up in an order that was constantly training you—not just teaching you—*training* you to recognize your limitations. (p. 41)

This is particularly revealing, because he wants you to give up your self and serve Christ…but he wants you to do it to *them*. Note how it doesn't say, "We want you serving Christ," but says "we want you serving Christ to us." This is not just about sacrificing yourself or following their teachings. It is about sacrificing yourself to the leaders of HH, because their "limitations" are different than yours. And they are the ones who show you what your limitations are.

He talks as though you are already beyond your limitations (which is a paradox he overlooks). He then talks about how you need to be within your limitations to find God. Keeping their teachings in mind, what this means logically is that he is talking about how you need to be within the Body and the limitations their standards put upon you to find God, because once you do that, you are a part of God (the Body).

This goes against Scripture from both sides.

> I am the vine; you are the branches. Whoever abides in me and I in him, he it is that bears much fruit, for apart from me you can do nothing.
> -   John 15:5 (ESV)

We have no power apart from Him. And yet…

> I know how to be brought low, and I know how to abound. In any and every circumstance, I have learned the secret of facing plenty and hunger, abundance and need. I can do all things through him who strengthens me.
> -   Philippians 4:12-13 (ESV)

We cannot expect to do anything ourselves, yet we must remember we can do anything through Him. Yet, Blair taught they were supposed to do what was required of them and they would not be serving God unless they stayed within their limits. This is because he did not truly want you serving God, he wanted you following his guidelines.

Though HH supposedly teaches all are part of the body, this also reveals how it is making the leaders the head of this body. They do it by following the frame of mind New Age often follows. Despite how it goes against what they often teach, they want to control everyone's actions one way and their thinking another.

***

The primary issue I see in HH outside its teachings, both from what friends of mine did, and what other members have told me, is the inconsistency of what they ask/require of each person. Not in how many tasks they give them to complete, but in how they restrain some more than those they seem to trust.

There are those I've seen join and devote to the community instantly with full dedication to their teachings. They often are allowed to continue living their lives in a relatively similar way as they did before. Others take time to be certain if they will stay, or have family members who are more hesitant. What then happens appears to depend on what the leadership thinks of their devotion and what they felt may hinder this member from following them with full dedication.

I have former friends still doing similar to what they did before they joined. I have others told to begin training in a whole new field. In this, I have noticed a pattern of it choosing those who show more strength in their devotion to, and faith in, HH to get to do more as they would choose. Those who were more hesitant to join or not fully accepting/understanding their teachings at first, appear to be the ones they do more to keep them under the stricter control of the leadership.

The clearest example of the first approach is in how Zach joined. As I explained, he is the one who did a lot of the teaching in our fellowship and was the one who drew others I know into HH.

Homestead has him in a position of leadership, because they know he is leading in the same direction as they were. His teachings were already close enough to theirs, and he was so quick to embrace theirs, so they have no reason to be of any concern he might start pointing people in a different direction than they want him to.

Seeing how his teachings made people more open to the concept of HH, I can also see how the life HH offered was enticing to those most devoted to him. With him constantly pointing to their sins and the ways of the world, they would want more than anything to find a way to be rid of temptation itself, the sin, but most of all the constant shame of seeing nothing but sin.

What I find infuriating about this is how HH and too many other cults take a passage saying to figuratively cut off your hand if it causes you to sin (Matt. 5:30), and instead of following what it says, they treat it as though it was saying you should cut off everyone's right hand if anyone's right hand causes them to sin.

Separation from anything, everything, anyone, and everyone that could cause sin is not possible until the new heaven and new earth are in place. But that is why their teachings, banners, slogans, etc. often speak of the "New Jerusalem".

As mentioned in passing in the previous chapter, HH has some similarities with Judaism. This is primarily in some of their celebrations and different activities they have. However, their talk of the "New

Jerusalem" is where it goes beyond that.

I have heard some speak of the members of HH as the current Israel—though they only claim this is the case due to the community they are a part of. This is because of the idea that they are the kingdom that needs to be built. This itself has its own paradoxes and conundrums, but they don't go into this much (as far as their teachings). This is more about their community and what their goals are.

When they do talk about it in messages and books, it is simply to show how they are to be this kingdom on earth. They do not explain much of what this means or how it is done. That is taught mostly by implication, word of mouth, or how the community is structured.

> …we are striving to become Jerusalem from above, which literally means, "city of peace," city of order and harmony, a "city set upon a hill," the "light of the world." And of "the increase of His *government* and peace there will be no end," for He will rule over it… (p. 8; *Coming into Orbit*)

The connection with Israel is one they have to make, but try to make as subtly as possible. If they simply claim to be Israel, which some of the more "extreme" leaders do, it does not go over well. Instead, they try to imply it more than say it. But they always push to follow the model given for Israel.

Treating themselves as the Body separate from the body, they go back to much of the Old Testament because that is what will fit best into their model. In the *Confession for Baptism and Communion*, it says,

I further confess that the New Testament cannot be properly

> understood apart from the vision and historical context provided by the Old Testament, especially its unfolding revelation of the One God of Israel. (p. 5)

The start of this sounds good, but this goes further than it says. They are not just talking about using the Old Testament to get the full picture. It becomes about this way of trying to connect with God as Israel. This is because the community they are trying to create is more like the nation of Israel than it is the body of Christ. It comes out more when you look at their social structure.

It is rarely mentioned, but when it is, it sticks out…

> Jesus's command to "be born of the Spirit" was also a call… given in order to arrange each person into a functioning place within the only kingdom that is "not of this world," the kingdom of self-giving love. It thus constituted an individual's commitment into the community of the committed, a commitment to give the rest of one's life to establishing this great conspiracy of caring on earth. (p. 169; *Life Against Death*)

This is another part they use in their general life and religious traditions, because it will get the members to follow them more than God, because their hope will be in the kingdom created now, instead of the coming eternal kingdom.

It is these traditions Blair said this about:

> This living tradition represents humankind's accumulated and lived wisdom… This kind of "tradition" can, then, be seen as life's staying power—the lifeline of human existence. (p. 145, 146; *Life Against Death*)

They do it this way on the daily living despite it rarely coming into the teachings so they can control both things of what they believe and how they live. They need to have things very structured. They have laws like those of the Old Testament. Some of them involving what you eat similar to that of the rules Israel followed. It can be seen in *Knowing God by Name* how they treat this community they are building the way Israel was:

> So the significance of the shift from Elohim level to the El Shaddai level of knowing God seems obvious: a new level of personal care has come to God's relationship with people and it is expressed in the blessings and fruitfulness of family and community in a new land-rooted setting that leaves urban Ur behind. (p. 81)

However, they have their differences and even have some with regards to your food beyond those of the Old Testament. Though they are usually not as dedicated to these rules because they will change them often, and certainly do not follow them consistently. They are always there.

To give an example, they had another, more innocent, similarity with the Mormons. They were against having coffee. They told everyone not to drink any. Yet, they changed this eventually and have opened their own coffee shop. (Which of these two were planned first is an interesting question to consider.) The question comes from another story which is more of a rumor, so I cannot tell it with certainty.

They did not allow coffee, but you also are not supposed to get food from outside what they produce themselves. I was told Blair had his own trailer separate from his home that he would often use as a sort of study to prepare his sermons and write his books. There was a stretch of times when he was out visiting different churches and locations when a bad smell started coming from his trailer.

For a while, no one did anything about it because no one other than Blair was allowed in it. However, the stench got so bad, some finally got inside to find the issue. What they found was a large number of old cups and bags from places like Starbucks and Panda Express getting old and causing the smell.

Again, don't know how true this is, but one I don't know the details of but find more confirmed by hearing it multiple places is that one rule they had against chocolate was removed because it was a favorite of one of leadership's children.

These are simple examples of how they give their own rules to the smallest things but are inconsistent with them.

However, they can push these rules dogmatically while they are in effect, and there are some even the leaders will hold to much more firmly themselves.

Following a framework similar to Judaism is used because it fits in better with the legalism they teach.

One thing I mentioned briefly before was a news story where they quoted a letter from a mother about accusations made by her son. The news article pointed out one part to show the abuse, while Homestead pointed out another to show the son was exaggerating it. However, what caught my attention, when I found a way to read it, came after these…

> I know that because of this belief system we spanked too hard, and for things that we shouldn't have. And now we know that it's not up to us to save our children by making them be good. So much fear. That fear made us do many harsh, hurtful things that our children and we must live with from now on.

This is wrong. It is pushing the parents to be harsher than necessary in their punishment. But what gets me is to see this is more evidence of a cult. The way the teaching forces them to punish so harshly out of fear of their children going to hell is how cults can work. It is not taught to make sure the children will obey their parents. The reason a cult will push this is because it is a way to drive the parents to do what will keep the children under the control of the cult's teachings. Thus, by such teaching, the leader(s) gain control of each family, and family member, that joins.

Again, their punishment always goes to an extreme. Whether it be mental or physical, they take it further than necessary (with one major exception). I have been told multiple stories of using this kind of punishment for simply asking the wrong kind of questions.

There have been family members outside the cult who talk to their friends' children, their nieces and nephews, or their grandchildren. I have heard there are multiple times they will be talking to the child of a cult member and the child may ask a simple question about why they do something or live the way they do, and the parent(s) will punish the child for raising the question.

They do whatever they can to keep control of how all of their members think—in other words they make sure their members think, "we are our Father's children, children who know no better, who have chosen to know nothing else."

However, they will not carry out as public and/or severe of punishments when the sin is something HH would want to hide and keep under wraps. There are some where they are more concerned with protecting the image of their community than they are with fixing the problems that come up.

This makes it so the sins (or even crimes) that go unpunished, or punished as little as possible, are the worst of them.

There have been multiple people arrested from HH for sexual crimes. Most of the time when this happens, the authorities find out later. Though HH always goes with no consequences because they know well what to say. They have a pattern of letting the authorities know what happened as soon as information starts spreading and questions may begin to rise. They will say they just found out, but there are multiple parts to some of these stories that make that not entirely true or highly suspicious.

Not only that, but multiple sources have told me the leaders of HH do in fact try to keep it under wraps by how they go about punishing and how they punish. Again, they will only turn them in if the story starts coming out.

This kind of thing happens in many cults. The leadership of a cult will often try to put some of the blame upon the one who was taken advantage of (usually a child). There are many testimonies of this happening within the JW's. They tell them it was something they did, said, etc. that drove the offender to do what they did. This happening most often to young ones makes it so they will feel so guilty and ashamed by what happened they will never want to speak of it. I have had a couple sources tell me similar things have happened at times at HH. Though, from what I've heard, the leadership has been more subtle in their wording and less severe in their method of the punishments, if it is true, it is still a similar method with a similar purpose that has no excuse, because it is for nothing but the sake of their own reputations.

When cults do this, it makes it so that those children harmed will not only never tell the story, but it also makes it so the parents will be just as quiet. Even if they see the issue, and maybe even leave, they know bringing it up inside or outside the cult will still bring great pressure and trial on their child.

Though everything I know, and most of what I have heard, tells me HH is not as extreme as some cults where the leader(s) use their authority to take advantage of the members sexually, I do see similar acts being done by different people in their community and almost supported in a more passive, or even unintentional, manner. It is by using this, they can claim their teachings and/or structure are not the cause of any problems. They thereby try to make anyone who comes against them look bad, or to simply hide from the accusations.

It is by this continuation of being hidden and silent that they are able to make the cult itself innocent or, at least, appear to be.

I can say this is a major problem that is found in every religious cult I have been looking at. Some cases are more severe than others, but all of them have examples of this. Many of them claim to want to create a society where temptations will not be able to get in, and when someone does make an error, it is their own personal issue, from going against the community in some way.

In the case of how HH's teachings work, it is their separation from the "Body" that caused the sin, thus they need the "communion" to be reunited with the Body.

Sometimes, it is the very thing they are doing of constantly putting people under such strict rules that drives particular members even harder to break them. It is the opposite of what Blair claims in *Knowing God by Name*:

> We can examine exactly how the Bible depicts people reaping the consequences of their freedom when they make the wrong choices. (p. 59)

He flips what is the issue. As Scripture talks about, the law was there not because it would prevent sin, but to show our nature and how rules cannot fix the problem.

> Let it be known to you therefore, brothers, that through this man [Jesus] forgiveness of sins is proclaimed to you, and by him everyone who believes is freed from everything from which you

> could not be freed by the law of Moses.
> -   Acts 13:38-39 (ESV)

The law caused more of the issue; it was not by freedom.

The final thing I want to discuss in this chapter is easily unnoticed. As I was just talking about the need for those who sin to reunite with the Body. it shows how they believe God's love is conditional.

One thing I found while reading one of Blair's books was a highly inaccurate view of the story of Job. It is one of my favorite books because of how much I learned, and found had not been told to me, when I read it for myself. Because of this, I was able to spot the errors more easily and with more certainty than most of Blair's other teachings.

One video I did on this topic is about how Blair treats it as though Satan knows nothing about God's love. This is clearly false. Satan was among the highest of God's angels and knew Him better than any of us do. However, what HH teaches shows me they know far, far less than him, and their thinking Satan knows little of it shows they know even less than I would have assumed.

Blair claims the challenge of Satan was against God's love. However, reading the book of Job, it is clear the challenge was solely against the faith and love of Job, not the love of God. Blair only pushed this direction to paint a particular image of Satan and of God.

This teaching was not coming from how Satan looked down on God's love. Instead, it came out of how Blair himself looked down on

God's love. Seeing it as conditional, he felt that what Satan wanted to show God would be a way of trying to make God make His own love more conditional to test the love of His followers further.

One friend, I will call Evan, was pulled into the teachings of HH, and one day the discussion of whether or not God's love is conditional or unconditional came up. We went into it for a while before I started to realize we were of the same opinion, but my friend did not realize HH simply changed what he was thinking "unconditional love" meant. He was treating it as though it meant God would show His love with nothing but blessing to everyone. At the same time, he was mistaking conditional love for what is unconditional love.

Blair wanted to make this story less about putting faith in God and His will, and more in how we need to be ready to fight through anything to "earn" the love of God.

What struck me about this was not so much what these teachings are (I kind of anticipated that), but how HH is using this.

Their love is conditional in each way it can be taken. Just as Blair's view of Job changed how conditional he believes God's love to be. They try to repaint the two forms of "love" to make it appear as though it should be "conditional". Having not fully joined, Evan would not realize how far they take it because he has not seen how they use that teaching.

Another friend was there for a short period of time but saw the issues. Yet, he wanted to stay in contact. When they saw what he disagreed with, they told him he could come to their church services, but he had to sit in the back and not have any contact with the members.

This is conditional love. Avoiding him is abandoning him, and if they truly did what Evan saw as conditional love, they would have "punished" one way or another, but not avoided.

What this shows is more of how their changing of the teachings is not just to make their own sound like something else, but to make those churches in disagreement with them appear to be teaching differently than they really are.

It is in this we can see the deception reaching another level. They are not just using it to make people let them in, nor to bring people in, but also to make people turn against those they were with.

This is why cults are seen in such negative light, and it is why they should be. But, just how bad is their effect and impact?

Chapter 6:

The Temptation of Ignorance

There is a popular quote used in so many ways in so many movies, books, sermons, etc. saying that the slyest trick Satan can pull is to convince us he does not exist. But no one can give exactly who started this saying because of how it has changed so many times with so many different words each time.

It is difficult to deny there is a lot of truth to this statement. Even those who are tricked by this lie admit it is a quote easily befitting of many of the best deceivers in this world. When it comes up in so many forms from different people, there must be some truth to it. However, you have to limit it. Claiming you know which trick is the cleverest is making too many assumptions that are unwise. Satan has many lies and tricks. We should never assume we have seen or heard of all of them. Each one is used at different times, in different ways, with different goals, and on different people.

If/when someone asks me if cults are his greatest tool, made of his slyest lies, his worst impact, etc., I will say it is his best for what task he uses it for. As I said, Satan is foolish, but he's not an idiot, and he knows different tools are better to use in different situations. It is among his greatest tricks, but it cannot be stated it's the cleverest of them.

Cults are and carry many lies, and too many don't consider their strength and uses.

We have already gone over how Homestead's teachings have similarities to multiple religions. Every cult does. Though they may twist them more or less from others and apply them differently, their teachings were drawn from another source or built with pieces of another teaching the leaders probably came out of.

When looking at these in multiple cults, it can seem their teachings and practices come from all over the place. So, it can be hard to find any one commonality found in all of them, in what they are trying to do with their teachings, or the lies they are using.

That is…until one considers what they claim that there could be a commonality in instead of just what the commonalities are.

When one looks at the religious cults and focusses on how they recruit and pull people in, they will find one of the most common characteristics is that they will claim to be Christian, show they are accepting of some of it, connected to Christianity, or to believe some form of Christianity—even when you find they don't believe these things after looking at their teachings more closely. They still have a common target of either drawing in or pretending to be part of the

Christian community.

There are clear exceptions to this. Usually, they are in other parts of the world. But when considering it, cults come out more often where there is no central religion. In these places, Christianity is their target.

This shows me why Satan finds Homestead's form of cult to be one of the better, if not the greatest, of his tools in leading specifically Christians away from the church.

HH is the cult that takes this to the extreme by two things. The first is by focusing their "recruitment" on those in a church. Many cults will target Christians, but they will not always go inside a church to get new members. HH does that, and only that.

So far, all of those I have spoken to from HH either grew up there, were there when it was starting, joined after being approached while in a church, or their family pulled them in. Basically, they were either approached at their church or are there due to family. So far, I have only spoken with one former member who I have found to be an example of any form of exception to this rule.

Some of the leaders of HH begin doing this by coming to a church in a way similar to visiting missionaries. Considering the rumors of Blair going across the country and speaking at many churches before starting HH, this makes sense. Everything about what they do and how they teach makes a model fit for the targeting of church goers.

Once they arrive, they will cause you to assume you are speaking with another brother or sister, and with everyone convinced of it, they know that most will completely trust them without any proof required.

It is a way of getting past all the doubts and hesitance that could come with approaching people on the street or knocking on their door.

My brothers and sisters were pulled in by Zach after he connected with HH. Homestead did this by coming to Zach and focusing on the commonalities they could see between what he was doing and what they did. They then had a prayer gathering at Zach's and many (even from out of town) came to join in. With these men from this community there putting so much trust in Zach, people were ready to trust them as well.

It was because of not just the trust my brothers and sisters had in Zach's teachings but also that he would not be deceived that they were willing to set aside any question that could come along about those from HH. The odd teachings were assumed to be misunderstandings or were ignored until they had time to think through it.

This is a method that is even more clever. They know they can pull far more in if they can bring a leader who already has a hold of these people over to embrace their teachings and community. The trust and reliance will already be in place. They just need to make sure they have a good hold on the end of the leash that is already there.

Why would a community such as this be so effective, and what would Satan's goals be in starting one?

Not only does a cult cause Christians, and others, to change their beliefs. There are plenty of religions, political groups and agendas, social causes, etc. trying to cause believers to put their priorities and views in the wrong place. A cult is about doing this by keeping them in a place where they are silent and deaf and every part of their lives are under the authority of the cult's leadership.

When believers only change their views, there are plenty of ways their views can be pulled back in the other direction if they read one of the right books, listen to a certain message, talk to the right friends, etc. In a cult, they are prevented from doing this and they are unable to learn much of what the other views are, let alone do any research to give them any consideration. What times they do get to, it won't do much, because they have been made to believe they do not know well enough. Even if something starts making them uncertain or raising concerns, how they are taught makes it so they must go to their leader(s) because they know the truth better.

HH puts its members in a place where they have leadership that wants them to be the "children who know no better," so they can have them following their teachings and their teachings alone. It is this boxing-in where they do not hear what others say about it or their own views, nor can they speak about their personal views. Thus, why I have heard them reciting the same message each time and they need a manual for answering to visitors' questions.

How can we expect them to think for themselves when there is no self to think? Control. It is what makes this fight so challenging. Satan wants all control. God granted us our selves. Satan wants to take it.

***

The second thing coming from Homestead's focus makes it so much harder for people to notice it than most cults. They are so centered on being "Christian" that they can narrow their wording down further than most cults are able to do due to their drawing in of people from far more varying religions and world views.

This is one of a few things they have found useful in keeping themselves cloaked as a cult. They sound so much more like a Christian church or ministry than most cults do.

It keeps the community full of those who are used to the kind of language they use. Even as they get used to new definitions, this will go unnoticed by too many because the statements have not changed. They only learned what these words "truly" meant.

This also makes it so the teachings can sound like the usual Christian churches to those outside.

But it goes even further than this. It also makes it so when they bring people in, and begin teaching them, the pot can start a bit warmer than most cults' pots and boil sooner.

It is why when my friends and I first started looking into HH we were concerned, but a little unsure. They don't want you to think about it. They want to sound Christian enough you won't question what they are teaching enough to see where the differences are. This is how we were so caught off-guard by just how quickly our friends were pulled in.

The sad thing is that this can be done by people who don't really want to deceive others. To some, it could be seen as nothing but a way to try and help others understand. They will see it as starting with the simple things and slowly getting to the more complex parts. They confuse the changes in definitions as details of the definition.

Others who follow them may have come to believe the differences are insignificant. They will think they are saying the same thing, and not acknowledge the changes.

Among leaders, or those not fully inside HH, it can be seen as a way to keep other churches from coming after them. They feel it is more of a protection of their members and/or their potential members.

There are many ways the members of a cult can do this unintentionally. However, there is a part of this that makes it so there has to be other intentions from someone higher up.

Some see it as a way to reveal the truth more fully to those outside their community. This is seen in multiple places within their baptismal agreement. When they start putting themselves above "other" churches is when the arrogance begins to take over until it is no longer about "helping" others, and more about showing their own confidence.

When this goes far enough, they begin to see it as a way to make the teachings "understandable" to those who do not have the standing, faith, or knowledge necessary.

When much of what they teach shows them as having more knowledge and understanding of Scripture than anyone else, there is no way of this not being the motive for some. If their teachings were correct, or what they truly believed, those who do this would be treated as having strayed.

It is something to remember when dealing with cults. They will do everything they can to convince you they have a good heart. And despite how many of them do, or even if none of them are intentionally doing it for the wrong reason, it does not change how some of them must have the wrong motive of arrogance, pride, and/or lust for power inside for it to be structured the way it is.

When so much of the world has been tricked into believing Satan does not exist, it is not hard to see the similarity within every cult and their methods of deceiving people. Even when they believe Satan exists, they will refuse to accept there's any way he can deceive them. The question is how this trick can be pulled so often and on so many within each of these cults and frauds.

As I was just describing, many assume they have a different motive than some of the leadership does. By being so innocent, they assume it is the same for everyone else. This can appear to be a bad assumption. However, within the teachings of HH it is just following what they've been taught. They are a part of this Oneness of the Body.

As I've mentioned before, my friends did not contact me about HH when they joined. Some of the other people they did not contact to try and draw them in to HH were some friends we have who came out of demonic or even satanic practices and came to accept Christ.

This can seem even more like they must know what is going on. However, they don't realize what they are doing because they probably see it as being gentle because even if what was being taught is true, those friends will be more on-guard about this kind of thing than others. Yet, this deception is not just self-deception. It is the indoctrinating of the cult's teachings and leadership.

It is how demons and Satan are often shown to trick people. They make the person think the darkest temptations, desires, or falsehoods they assume are their own thoughts when at times they're not. That the strange dreams, disturbing fantasies, etc. come from themselves. Or the teachings and indoctrination they are hearing from false prophets are so indirect, they believe they came to the conclusion themselves, not from the teaching of someone who is trying to trick them.

Some cults hide Satan and the demonic, while they are following this example. As it says in Scripture,

> And what I am doing I will continue to do, in order to undermine the claim of those who would like to claim that in their boasted mission they work on the same terms as we do. For such men are false apostles, deceitful workmen, disguising themselves as apostles of Christ. And no wonder, for even Satan disguises himself as an angel of light.
> -   2 Corinthians 11:12-14 (ESV)

But Satan, and false prophets, will at times do the opposite as well. He will try to convince people that he cares. There are people who knowingly follow Satan, because they believe a lie that says Satan is fighting for them. This same thing happens in the cults when the community tries to portray itself as being "loving".

When one looks at many cults and talks to those who joined, there is a story more common than any other. Former members or potential members will visit and be admiring how loving the people in that community were to them—how much special attention they gave to the visitors, and what they would do for you.

It is one of the first things I am told by those who visit HH and have not considered what they teach closely enough, or decide to set it aside. They visit and find the people to be so caring and inviting that they feel like I must misunderstand what the community is doing and how good the people there are. They have trouble seeing how such nice and caring people could be part of a cult—they never consider if those people could have been deceived.

If you bring up a cult, people often think of those communities as dark, strange and scary places. However, when one visits, the community makes sure your time there is as pleasant as possible. The last thing they want is for you to have any room for suspicions of what they are really about. (Whether they do it deceptively or honestly.)

This can happen anywhere, but in a cult, it is far more extreme. It is a balancing act. Once again, for most there, it is not necessarily because they are trying to trick or deceive those visiting. It is not even what would, in most churches, be a "sales pitch".

Most often, it is because they want to show their "love", because of what they have been taught there and what they believe they have already experienced. They want you to experience it as well. They overdo it, in a sense, not because they feel it will take that much to make the person believe it is a good place but to make them see what they believe their community is.

When one is in a place like this and sees it as such a bright light, they feel they really need to strive to portray that well enough for those visiting to understand what their community truly is. Thus, they can be putting on an act without thinking they are—making the community look like something it isn't. To them, they are trying to make their weak selves look like the community that is so perfect.

In reality, what we witness is them lying to themselves, and we are only overhearing it.

Cults always hide themselves with what we have discussed from the start—the definition of a cult.

Why? How? That is always a part of what a cult is. They are supposed to be another religion, organization, cause, university, training facility, etc.

To put it plainly, a cult is an extreme form of fraud. They are trying to steal everything, not just your money—your career, your labor, your property, your loyalty, your identity. your family, your self.

This fraud can initially come from a person seeking money,

power, or even worship. Other times, it can come from a person who has already been deceived themselves, and they want to "help" others. It can come from a group of people who found a commonality it appears no one else has, and instead of realizing it is because they are mistaken, they want to show it to others. Whatever may cause the initiation of this group, it always has a fraudulent image lighting the way.

As I said earlier, they can each seem so unique because there is always something that is different. It is the way this uniqueness is treated as being a part of a common religion or practice that makes them a fraud. They always want to be unique, but they don't want to be entirely unique. They want to be a unique sect of an existing belief system.

This cloaking works in part because of there being so many denominations and religions. They try to make the newcomers see them as another sect of Christianity, or as similar as possible to another denomination. It makes it so those they approach have no reason to be on guard about the most crucial teachings, because they feel they can assume those won't be changed.

If they were, how could it be Christian…

It is this assumption and circular reasoning that the teachings do not exist that keeps those joining from looking closely enough to see them.

There is an assumption made about Satan by far too many churches. They believe he works within the ways of this world, and then, they assume this means he leaves us alone. But other churches realize the wolves will always try to sneak in amongst the sheep.

Though some are guarded on this front, there are times it goes even further. There are times you will have a pack of wolves pretending to be those sheep within a far safer pen and under the "true" shepherd(s). They will lure you in and lock you inside while claiming it is for your safety or even make you believe the lock did not do anything and show why you have no reason to leave.

Then, there are times they will slowly remove the costumes bit by bit and draw everyone else to make themselves look like them.

This is where I see a more defining characteristic of a cult. It makes leaving much harder. It is after this that you will find the other sheep must be in the same costumes the cult leaders were in. This means that if you escape the pen, you must wander on your own. You will be lost in a dangerous forest, and you cannot trust any who want to help. Then, finding there is no one outside the pen you feel safe with and no way of keeping yourself safe, out of fear, you run back to the pen.

In the pen, there can be nothing but your allies. As you have been convinced of for so long, Satan cannot be there.

One of the slyest tricks Satan can pull is to convince us he does not exist… until he can find a way to convince us only he is the shepherd.

Chapter 7:

The Leash Without a Collar

There are many discussions about how to get someone out of a cult. Many of the methods can be useful. There are many ways to try and get people to realize what they are a part of. The hard part is often first getting to where they can be spoken with.

Given many times friends and I have tried speaking with those who joined, I have to say HH seems to have started doing their best to keep us from speaking with each other without a mediator. We have compared notes after multiple short conversations. When they were in town to take care of some loose ties, some of us wanted to try meeting up with them to discuss things. As we were in contact with them, many would ask to meet up and when they would be available. What they would say about what they were doing and who they had heard from was told differently based on who they were speaking with.

Sadly, this should be a flag, but few who joined see it. I have never heard a pastor tell people to call and have him come over before trying to have a chat with JW's or Mormons who knock at your door. In a cult, they may do this even if you are having a basic chat with friends who go to another church.

HH does this, and from what I've heard, they often do not let it be a conversation between you and your friend. It is a conversation between you and the one overseeing it.

When you do get a chance to talk to them, the conversation often comes to an agreement because what you point out about their teachings will bring you both to agreement, if you do not know the language they have been taught to speak.

So, how does one get through to them?

Before I get into this, I have to bring up one of those very rare times I mentioned I would suggest to take another route than Hassan.

One thing he brings up a few times in *Freedom of Mind* is trying to think the way they think to practice for asking questions. I would advise against this.

I can see the benefit in some cases, and I see that benefit as important. However, I see a danger as well.

Too often it is better not to be able to think the way they think. Their thinking is often illogical. It is good to understand how it works, and being able to see what's making them come to the conclusions they are. But when you try to think that way yourself, you can unintentionally be making yourself think illogically.

So, yes, understand how they are thinking differently, but no, do not force yourself to think that way as well. There may be a good way to do this, but be certain you are not fully taking on their way of thinking and throwing your reasoning to the wind. It still needs to be there to make sure you are doing this properly.

I could also see this strategy being more properly used in some other debates and discussions, but it is because we are speaking about cults that are all about brainwashing that I would be cautious. As a believer, I would even be cautious how this is used in other situations.

I personally wrote a devil's advocate paper in college where I tried to see how well I could argue for atheistic evolution. I kept myself reasoning logically, so I did not come to the same conclusions they would have, but I was able to figure out what they would probably say in certain situations and even found some potential arguments I would not have anticipated otherwise. At times, I pushed too hard to think their way, and I would find myself lost where I was. It would bring confusion, and I would have to reset my train of thought to keep it in focus.

So even though it can be useful outside of cults I would still be cautious how much you force yourself to think like they do. I would say just think logically and see what you can find of arguments they might use.

With this in mind, first make sure you have a general idea of what they really teach. However, make sure you remember this is not always so you can convince them otherwise, but so that you can understand what they are saying and stay firm where you stand. (I will discuss why the goal is rarely to convince them later.) Until you know what they are saying, you cannot have a conversation.

However, this preparation is the easy side of it. Finding the way to get into contact with them is the hard part. And the easiest way is the way I would take a firm stand against.

There are some things I've seen and heard people either want to try or are trying that I would advise against. I want to touch on these and the issues they can cause before I get into the better way to handle the situation.

Several I have spoken to or heard from think they should try and get their friends to meet them outside of the cult and then have a couple other people with them, or even have an intervention. Others will try and stay in contact by acting as though they are in agreement with some/most of HH's teachings. A few may even think of pretending to join the cult so they can "penetrate" to pull them out. Others will consider telling them they need to meet with them for some kind of emergency or urgent issue. They feel that getting them to meet up but then talk with them about the cult and the issues they have with it would help. At times, these methods may seem to work in helping the friends/family hear what is going on, only to find out they were only pretending to get out. Some times they will leave as soon as they learn of your intentions and never be willing to be in contact with you again. Other times, done the right way, it has a very minor chance of working. However, each of these has one major issue.

They are each reliant upon a lie.

Some of my contacts who left Homestead do not speak up about HH so they can remain in contact with their family members. They don't come against HH or try to support it. They also avoid talking to family members about it what they can. That kind of situation is not what I am talking about in these cases. My concern is when someone acts as though they believe HH and/or are willing to join/rejoin to trick them.

If you use methods such as these to try and reach your friends and family, it can cause more issues. At some point, even if the process you use will start to work, it has to come to where they find out you were lying. When this happens, they will see it as proof of everything the cult has told them, because the cult was right about how we lie to them. But even if they have been questioning things and are looking at the situation more reasonably, both you and them will have to admit you lied. No matter how either of you see it, this will create an additional problem to fix. I say avoid any of these methods as much as possible.

There are times it can get to a point where forcing an intervention may seem more necessary as a last resort. Yet, Hassan even insists that you need someone experienced in such things to do it properly. I would not say doing it with help is an absolute no, but make sure you are certain it is all you can do, or it is the only thing that could work, and you have someone who can help you do it right. Make sure they are not just someone who has experience in this, but also has knowledge of this cult, their teachings, and are on the same page as you spiritually.

However, even in this, I will insist you need to be as honest as possible. This is what makes it so hard to find a way of not just contacting them, but making that contact get through.

This is why I think HH is possibly among a short list of what I would consider to be the cleverest of cults when it comes to their method of recruiting.

Many will collar their followers to identify them as one of theirs and then put them on a leash to not let them get too far from the premises (this distance is literal and metaphorical). Due particularly to recent things that have happened, HH is too clever for this. They will not give you a collar.

What leash they do use is primarily of a mental kind of restraint, not physical. Instead of letting the dogs do as they wish while having a leash to keep them at a set distance, they let them go as often as HH sees it is within reason (and they trust the individual enough), but lately, HH often will send someone else with them to "help" them (dependent on the member who is on the trip). They put this "helper" there as though they are following them. However, by the teachings this member would be following, the leash on them mentally is far shorter than the one they are led to believe they have on their helper.

It is similar to the way Mormons and JW's go out from door to door. They always go with one who has been taught well, and one who is newer. It can seem to the newer member they are there to help them and support them, but the ultimate goal is more to direct than encourage and help.

In the cults like the JW's, it is to prevent what the other person says from causing the "weaker" to think for themselves. It is to keep that collarless leash on their minds.

When HH does this, they're rarely going out to witness. This makes it even more careful and deceptive.

This is also why being as unconvincing as possible can be the most convincing.

Cult members are used to being constantly taught. They are used to having ideas constantly forced on them. Usually, when we try to give good arguments, they only hear what they have already been told repeatedly so that they are ready to fight back.

Side note: if you do find this may help, meet up with them, and if there is a mediator, they may be unable to discuss things with you. But make sure you talk to them and do it lovingly and with as calm a demeanor as possible. This mediator will be there to try and get in the way of the communication. Though he may be able to restrain what they say, he will only have what control he has over you because you give it to him. Keep the conversation directed at your friend or family member, not at the one trying to keep them leashed. The point of posing the questions is to get them thinking, not to get the answers. So, never push for an answer, and if they don't respond, let them stay silent. Pushing will only cause the mediator to do more to make sure your loved one did not listen to you.

Still, it can be good not to be too quick to start using logical arguments. In the case of HH, it is especially unwise to go by logic until you are certain they have started reasoning through things, and even then, it is best to be careful not to push too fast or too hard.

As so many current members and former friends told me when I tried to reason with them, and said in their testimonies, their logic made them question things. But they had an experience. This causes any reasoning to be of little to no use, because they already chose to throw that out the window because they wanted to join for another reason.

This causes everything normally used in confronting them on the issues to be useless. They had turned their backs on using reasoning willingly when they joined. It can make most methods of trying to show someone how they were tricked futile.

Note: one exception to this can be showing them the context and meaning of knowing by their fruit. It being the one thing they use to excuse their own abandonment of comparing it to Scripture, this is the only part some may be put into a corner with. Yet, too many will have enough faith in HH for even this to impact them.

If you are in this situation, talk to them but don't let the conversation go in a direction that has anything to do with debate or argument.

Instead, use what HH used…love them.

As is heard time and time again in the stories of those who visited a cult or joined then left, they felt so loved when they first visited HH, and that is why they surrendered logic and self. However, when a place, such as HH, is pushing for a conditional love, this feature that drew them in is going to be temporary.

When those outside the community show a love that is unconditional, this can be what will make them question what they are a part of. It will show them this place is not the perfect community they assumed it to be. It is by revealing the issues with what first drew them in that can make them begin to question things. They may realize they had a more real form of what they joined for even before they did join.

It is a challenge, because there is no way of knowing when something will happen to reveal the issue. However, I would say try to talk to them as much as possible—until you find they are starting to ask questions, then it is better to be more patient and let them contact you instead of only you contacting them. This could let them have more time to think and be far more ready to listen when you have a conversation.

If you keep coming at them with love, they can start to see it is not only HH that can always be there for them.

This leads to what can be an immensely difficult challenge. I will say, this is something I have had extra experience in with more than just those coming out of a cult.

I have spent time with people not only coming out of cults, but also dealing with depression, anxiety, and even suicide. I have had times I have been called in the middle of the night because someone is ready to end it. I do respond differently, depending on the person and how sincere I can tell they are, but it was my first priority to be ready to encourage them when they needed it.

This is one thing to be ready for. If you are constantly contacting them, you never know when the time will come that they start to have questions, or something forces them to see it from another angle. When that comes, do not turn them down. No matter the situation, talk to them as long as they are going through the problems in their mind and you are able. Any time you delay or decline, they can see that as showing you were not authentic either.

In other cults, it is more about what they teach. Occasionally, someone in a place like HH may recognize something that will cross the line for them. In these cases, carefully questioning things can be more useful. However, I have heard some make suggestions I will disagree with.

I was suggested to view one video where Michael Heiser made a suggestion for talking to those in cults. What he said was a great suggestion for talking to those of other religions. There may even be the occasional cult where it could help. However, for the majority of cults I would advise against this method.

He suggests asking them to convince you of something they hold to most strongly. He says to ask them to get you past an issue. In talking to someone of another religion, this can help, but when talking to someone of a cult, they are not trying to reason with you. They are showing you what they "know" to be the truth, not truly trying to convince you logically of it.

In my opinion, asking them to show you what they already have decided is only going to make them push to convince you of it and make them more used to saying what they have already come to believe. They will not try to reasonably change your mind. They are only going to keep coming at you again and again until you accept or give up.

This can work to an extent if you are asking about things outside their beliefs or ask about things you already agree with them on. The first can get to where issues that are less debatable may lie, and they will have less reason to be on the defensive and nothing to argue with. They will start to look at what is happening in their community more honestly. When this leads them to start looking for examples instead of just claiming assumptions, they will be seeing for themselves. If it is something you agree on, it will show them you are not just their opponent. What lies they may have been told about you being against the truth will start to crumble.

This also helps, because it will make it something you don't have to force. It is not something you will have to explain. Once they start trying to answer the question or see you are not their opponent, they can start seeing it for themselves.

The second question will be even more useful in those cults with a tighter collar and leash. It will bring more opportunities to show them you are not against them. They will see you are willing to admit they are correct when they are. They will find that you are not attacking them unreasonably—as the cult leaders will be telling them you do. This can give them a reason to listen to what you say, and some of the real challenges may start to be heard.

However, what I would suggest to aim for most is asking about what they ignore. Don't point solely toward what they agree with. Only use that as a way of opening the door to these questions.

In the case of HH, if I came across someone who was drawn in more by the teaching than the society, I would point to the passages that they contradict, particularly those contradicting their practices more than their teachings, and ask what they think it means. If they try pointing toward a passage HH often uses, 95% of the time, one could simply read the context and then ask them how it can mean that. But try not to let them get around the question. Go back to it each time they try to lead away. I would suggest to do this patiently by not stopping them immediately but redirecting after responding to what they tried to use.

Making them face the things the leadership tries to hide of Scripture would be a better way to cause them to second guess. If you try to give them just logical reasoning, that will not work well because they are not going by their own reasoning. They are going by the reasoning of their leadership. But when you can show something in the Bible that goes against their teaching, there will be less they can do. Their only way around it would be to admit they don't put the Bible first or as inerrant. This will even go against what HH claims to believe.

However, the approach of this does depend highly on the cult, their method of teaching, and how the people are drawn in.

***

Following this approach, there is another useful tool.

One suggestion by Hassan I was hesitant on at first, but it led my mind to something that could be extremely useful after adding one more step Hassan did not put there.

Hassan often suggests posing hypothetical questions. This can be useful in particular cases, but one thing I would add to suggesting it is to be cautious how you pose the question, depending on the person, the cult they are in, and where they are in the process of questioning.

One of the questions he suggests is to ask them what the leadership could do or teach that would make them leave. At first, I did not like this question, because I know many would not go the direction he mentions. I know some who would say it would not, or could not, happen and refuse to consider the hypothetical as possible.

However, thinking about this, I realized how useful this could be. If they say this, just ask, "Do you think they are inerrant?"

Particularly for my friends under the teaching of HH, this would put them in a spot where all three answers (yes, no, I don't know) will put them in a corner where they have to flee or admit there is an issue.

If they say, "Yes," they are admitting to seeing the words of their leadership as equal to the Word of God. If they say, "No," then they are admitting the hypothetical is not impossible. If they say, "I don't know," they will be admitting they did not consider the question.

Though the effectiveness of this and many other questions would depend on the teachings of the cult itself, in most cases there is one topic that will point in the right direction.

It is good to make it so some questions point to the past—previous to their joining of the cult. When pointing to what they experienced in the churches or communities they were a part of before they were recruited, it can bring out more of their selves. It can remind them what it was like so they can make a more honest comparison between what things were like before and after.

These need to be specific. Don't let them look at it generally. Try to discuss or ask about the details. If they give it enough thought, they can start to see things were not as bad as the cult made them believe they were, or they will find some of what they saw as so unique to the cult were not as unique as they thought.

There is one thing I would suggest needs to be kept in mind more than anything else, when it comes to getting people out of a cult. It points to what is necessary whatever the approach may be in that particular case. It is something counteracting everything the cult has been doing since they first started to join.

Let them think for themselves.

When you ask a question, their response can often go nowhere, or they may not even admit to themselves you asked a question. Don't let this happen. Yet, don't force it too harshly. Only do enough they will acknowledge you gave it to them.

Cults are always indoctrinating their followers. They do it by getting the members to stop thinking. When you pose questions, make sure you don't push too hard or fast. Give them time. Even if they answer quickly, wait to see if they will say more so it can get them to this point where they are actually thinking.

If you do as Heiser suggested, I fear, and have seen it before, they will only be reciting what they've already been told. What "they" say in this situation is rarely what *they* think. They need something to take their thoughts in a direction where they don't have a recited answer. Once they get there, you have to be sure you don't push. If you stay silent for a time, they have a chance to be forced to consider what was just said and to see that hole you brought them to.

The one thing I hear without end from members or supporters of HH is how I need to stop judging the people. They will constantly point out what good and loving people they are and how I need to stop treating them with such hate.

One friend I had called me and used this. I then told him that I thought the people there were great individually. I told him how I was not against the people there, but what they are being taught. I started talking about how frustrating I find it that the people can be so quickly judged by those outside when they're the ones being told the lies.

When I finished indirectly arguing how HH was judging their members more than I was. He went silent for a while, and I tried not to prevent his thinking.

This is what happens almost every time I am judged for judging. If I can tell they are definitely a devout member trying to accuse me, I may simply mention the hypocrisy of what they're saying. I will just ask them why they are judging me for judging. However, if I can see they really care about the people and are upset by what I'm saying, I always try to show them my concern is against the teachings and for the people they are claiming they want to defend. It will often put them in a corner.

This makes it so it can also be useful to start conversations about other false religions and cults.

They will be against them just as much as you are. Pointing out their faults is something they will be as eager to assist in. If, once this kind of conversation has gotten going, you can pose a question which indirectly will point back on them, it will put them between a rock and a hard place.

I had a question to pose with Evan, when I found myself in a position where I could get another chance of making a connection with him. However, I went down this road by bringing up a passage in Zechariah 13. It speaks of the false prophets leading many astray. I was mentioning a recent Bible study we had looking at it and considering how there are so many false teachers and false prophets in a similar position today.

I could do nothing more than mention it too him, because I could see the tension rise. I did not say anything more. I did not ask anything.

I could tell something was wrong when we left. I hope this confirms that it was bothering him in some way and got through enough to make him think for himself. I pray this will continue sitting in the back of his mind to make him ponder it.

HH tries so hard to appear to be a Christian community. They don't want those outside their community to truly understand their teaching. So, when someone points out issues in their teachings, those who truly know and follow HH's teachings are put in a corner. They have no room to say they believe the same thing, but they also are hesitant to give any real logic for why your beliefs are wrong because it will show they do follow these teachings they don't want people to know about.

This is what has caused some of the most circular and illogical discussions I've ever had. They were in the comments on different videos I put on my YouTube channel. When it went this direction, I could tell these are the kind of people it is futile to discuss the issues with. The only reason I did in these cases was because the discussion would be more public and could potentially reveal the truth to those who are visiting the webpage.

Outside this kind of situation, it is always more beneficial to keep the argument from continuing than it is to debate no matter where they are in the cult or what kind of cult it is. If you ask questions or make comments on things about the cult, them, or what is happening in their life outside the cult, that can cause trouble for their perspective. Either they will feel like they don't know enough to respond, or they will, deep down, know there is an issue and try to avoid any kind of debate as well.

This can make the discussion go where you would really want it to go—to be nothing but a conversation between friends.

Of course, no matter what the cult is, the best way to get someone out does depend not just on which cult it is but a great deal on the individual as well. It is the individual that needs to be brought back out. And the individual is what the cult was trying to eliminate. This makes it so their personal perspectives can be most important in this.

There is one thing within this that could be an interesting tool: their preferences—particularly their preferences about things they no longer have anything to do with now that they are in a cult. Maybe movies, books, music, or games. Perhaps vacations, theme parks, and other activities. Whatever it is, stirring up their former opinions (by agreement or argument) can start to bring out their former selves.

You could try bringing up current news stories about politicians or celebrities you know they followed or were against previously. Maybe you could mention someone they knew a long time ago that you recently heard about or bumped into. Telling them a story about something that happened to you somewhere they have not been in a while. This will get them to think about their past even further, and it may get their selves exploring more than just their former opinions.

There could be many other things like this. They are useful because they will not be something you mentioned to point out issues with where they are. It will have nothing to do with the problems of what they are taught. It is where their defense may be lowest—memories.

As long as you don't push further if they asked you not to talk about those things, it cannot hurt to give it a shot and still point to it every now and then.

As I've mentioned, the last option is an intervention. This is extremely difficult to pull off. There has to be a way of getting someone to take a step away from a cult to visit someone or join some kind of activity. Their family and/or friends then pull them away to somewhere where they can prevent the cult member from contacting the other members. Then they will try to show them the issues in what they have become a part of.

As I've said, this may work. However, I personally have major issues with it. As I mentioned before, lying will cause trouble, and this method, too often, begins with nothing but deception. But I have to bring it up again, because there is an angle to it that makes me feel its usual use can be missing a crucial part.

It is misused, because it can still work at times. What can make this work is how short a time this lie will last. The issue then becomes who you will try to convince them to trust. There are times this is made to convince them of the fraudulence of the lies they have been told.

This brings out the problem with this method. It can cause those who want to get the member out of the cult, to use the same processes and means as the cults used.

You will be separating them from all of the false teachings, the same way the cult will separate them from what they call the "false teachings". You may start forcing them to listen to your way of looking at things and not letting them think through it, just as the cults do. You will be putting them in a place where they may start taking in everything you say because it is being demanded of them and not truly because they have come to the conclusions themselves—just as the cults do in brainwashing them.

The second issue I have with this kind of action is how the situation and setting can lead those involved to act and talk in a way that will have the opposite of the effect being sought.

As can be imagined, the tensions will be extreme in many of these cases. The tension is high enough when it is nothing but a phone call. Being put in a place like this is going to make it escalate. This will put both sides on guard and the aggression higher, and either side will make the other continue to go deaf to what is being said.

What the people usually need in this case is not for family and friends to correct them. They don't need family to show them the truth. They are not the problem.

What the members need is to be reintroduced to their selves. They need to learn to think again, instead of reciting. They need to learn to decide what *they* believe, not what They believe. They need to learn how their minds were silenced, not just how they were deceived. There is a reason everyone I've spoken with who left after realizing what was wrong were able to—because they found a time and place they could think for themselves.

This is why a method of intervention can work as a last resort. However, that is only if, instead of trying to convince them to listen to one liar instead of another, they are helped to find a way to regain trust of their own thinking. The family and friends need to spend time with them and show them they care. They need to be shown what made others concerned—not that they knew better.

It means they need to realize you are not asking them to believe you. You are not trying to convince them yourself. You are not the one trying to lead them on another leash. You are letting their minds roam free, only care about them having this freedom, and want to be sure they know what they believe.

As an author, I can say it is a way of carrying the concept of "show, don't tell" beyond its use in fiction that is needed no matter what method may be used to pull someone out of a cult. Instead of claiming you know the truth better than them, you need to let them see reality for themselves to begin reobtaining their selves.

No matter the method you choose, there is one thing I will say is necessary even in its own exception. And this can be applied in helping others with almost any issue of this sort—beyond just getting them out of a cult…

Patience.

Even in times where you may need to resort to this more questionable method and act quickly, that first step may need to be swift but you will need the patience for what comes after the process begins.

Every way out of a cult will be trying for anyone involved in the process. I had a couple friends come out only months after joining HH, and I attempted to talk to them as much as possible and spend as much time with them as I could to help them through the trials and thought processes they were dealing with. However, once they start to see the lies, it can be crucial to allow them to determine the direction the conversations go. Even though it can be easier when they have already decided to come out on their own, it is still going to be a challenge.

It is the required endurance that is crucial.

Looking back on what happened when I first came to be part of the fellowship I am in now, changing some insignificant views when I read through Scripture for myself often took time. I would have to keep going back to the passages to be certain I was looking at it clearly, and remind myself of what it said. Imagine how much harder this would be for one who is coming out of a cult where they have been truly brainwashed.

That's why there's a whole lot more to this than just getting someone out.

Chapter 8:

Safety Is Not of This World

One thing I personally find frustrating is when I hear that idea in some AA groups having people always start anything they share by saying their name and, "I am an alcoholic," no matter where they are in the process of getting off of it. What bothers me about this concept is how they are being told to admit defeat before they are attacked again.

I tried being part of some varying forms of support groups to help others after my own difficulties with things such as depression, anxiety, and different kinds of temptations (suicide, temper, etc.) However, there were some groups that did nothing but reinitiate some of my struggles. I would find a way to overcome something to the point it was not bothering me and its attacks were barely noticeable, then they would bring it up with me again in some of these meetings. It would only cause me to fall back into the trap of listening to it.

Getting off drugs is always seen as such a difficult and trying process. Having personally been through withdrawal from getting off of certain medications, I can testify to you there is only one thing I have experienced that is more difficult to endure than that, but there are many similarities to other struggles that would not normally be seen as addictions.

Coming out of a cult has its similarities to this process. However, when someone is coming out of a cult, it can be far worse.

Constantly identifying as an alcoholic is something I may not like the idea of, but I do see the point they can try to make with it along side the potential issue it could cause to be too careless. However, I can tell you with certainty, it not only has places it will cause more trouble, but also, this kind of approach would be the worst thing to do to one trying to get away from their addiction to a cult.

As I've said and will continue to push, a cult is all about taking away your identity. If you want to truly get out, you have to find your self again. You must be rid of the fake identity they gave you.

When getting off a drug, you will have these times of withdrawal on occasion. If you stumble and go on another high, you need to get back off it. When coming out of a cult, it can be similar. However, it can also be far more constant and have little to do with you stumbling.

A drug plays most with your mind during that high or time of withdrawal. The former teachings of a cult will be haunting you much more consistently as a subconscious response to everything else you hear or read. Even some of the things I heard Zach say at times still toy with my mind from time to time for me to question them, and I never chose to follow it.

The reason this is particularly bad for those coming out of a cult is because the leadership would immediately point to how what you are feeling at these times is the "Spirit", "Way", "Truth", etc. pointing out to you your misunderstandings. It's because those indoctrinated will not listen to themselves that they will immediately be drawn to listen to the voice that is not their own.

It is this constant battle always there no matter where in the process someone is at that makes it an extreme draw trying to force you back in similar to an addiction. However, I'm sure most would agree that no one dealing with it should say, "I am so-and-so, and I'm a Homestead Heritage member." What can start to change this battle is when they hear that way of thinking whispering to them and they can speak up and state, "It was never me following them, and they don't have control of my self anymore."

Never accept defeat before the battle starts.

Once you can get through to a member of a cult, and get them to question any aspect of the cult, remain patient, but as soon as a current member of a cult decides they want to leave, the important thing is for them to do it without hesitation. The worst things they could do at this point is to confront others or let certain people know before they leave. Instead, they need to walk away, and then, if they insist, try contacting their friends, or the cult, from a distance to let them know.

Cults know plenty of ways to hold onto their members if they start considering to leave. In order to prevent a quick departure, HH has this in their baptismal agreement:

> I further agree that I will not take such a step of separation apart from honoring God by pleading with leaders as fathers…to bring complete resolution to any such issues before leaving and, finally, if all else fails, committing in both spoken and written words my reasons for leaving… (p. 126)

They can use (often indirectly) the teachings of Jesus when He tells us we need to confront someone, and then go with another person, before bringing them before the body to try and push this. However, this is there only to make sure no one will leave without the leadership of HH having a chance to try and keep them in the cult. This has nothing to do with what that part of Scripture is talking about in correcting an individual. Be ready to explain this to them if such an argument comes up for why they need to speak with the leadership of the cult first.

Despite what teaching of the cult may be used to keep them from leaving too quickly, the union the member has gained with those in this community is what is most likely to keep them there. The leadership is often aware of this. They know it is by this they will have the easiest way of being able to keep a hold of any members who are considering leaving the cult.

If someone decides to leave, this is why they need to do it without saying anything. Those they speak to may try to "reason" with them. They may try to make them feel some kind of guilt for abandoning them. Or there could be no real response, but the indoctrination will cause them to doubt themselves once again if they receive no attacks from those they speak to (though this may only mean they will be approached later, it will give time for those who would try to change their mind to get their chance).

The way a cult like HH is aware of, and attempts to prevent, potential ways for a member to leave is why this massive document has to be inspected and signed before they are allowed to become a member.

It is because of these issues that former cult members always need new or former friends there to help when and after they come out. The "fellowship" is what they were in the cult for. Being without one is part of what can make them run back, but again, always keep in mind being a friend could mean nothing more than being there for them. Not hanging on them.

Try to let them know you're there and available, but never push further than letting them know you are able to respond to them. They need, more than anything, to think for themselves. And when you do speak, above anything else, give them hope and encouragement…no matter what. Even in the issues that come up or problems you need to address, give them hope alongside the confrontation. They will need something else to hold onto so they can let go of the fear that acts as their chain.

As we have been seeing in everything we are looking at, this is all about a fight against the fear the cult uses to confine them. Hope is what they need to constantly be reminded of. They need to see the places and things they can benefit from outside of the community they left. With fear showing up often, they will see less distinction between what is inside and what is outside.

The Bible says, "The fear of the Lord is the beginning of knowledge," (Proverbs 1:7 ESV) and that's what it is—the *beginning*. It is only the start, and it is only the fear of Him. It is once this fearing of Him fully replaces the fearing of men, or even one's self, that brings wisdom.

This requires for one to stop fearing others and the false teachings of the cult leaders, and that can be one of the most difficult parts in the process.

Every cult I have looked into so far does so much to cause the members to fear themselves, the leadership, and also the entirety of the outside world. It is understandable how anyone who may try to leave them will suffer even more fear.

Being rid of fearing themselves is the first step, which is why they need to begin thinking for themselves and finding who they were. As they start doing this, things can start to become much different than they anticipated. Some things will get easier. Other things will not be so daunting, because they can now handle it themselves.

The next can be finding not to fear all leaders. The Bible says to fear only God—not men.

They need to realize what it is truly like to have a helper who is not holding that hidden leash. They need to realize what a true leader is based on the Bible:

> A dispute also arose among them, as to which of them was to be regarded as the greatest. And he said to them, "The kings of the Gentiles exercise lordship over them, and those in authority over them are called benefactors. But not so with you. Rather, let the greatest among you become as the youngest, and the leader as one who serves. For who is the greater, one who reclines at table or one who serves? Is it not the one who reclines at table? But I am among you as the one who serves."
> -   Luke 22:24-27 (ESV)

This is the part of Scripture a cult will twist and/or reject more quickly than any other. Even if some of the cult's teachings may be adjustable, the rejection of this is the only thing that keeps it together as what it is.

Those who leave a cult will often be in a place where this kind of leadership feels like a paradox to them. Many I have spoken with who left HH (even some who left other legalistic churches) stay separated from any gatherings because they need to keep from being under someone else's control. By the leash HH uses, the distinct line between "helped" and "controlled" has been blurred for them.

It is this need for learning how a leader can be more of a servant that is a hard step for them to take. That is too often what a cult leader talks as. Most of the time he tries to keep a humble demeanor. However, as soon as he is in a place where he is going to do something with his leadership, his demeanor completely changes.

If one rejects a cult they were in, it takes them realizing the leader(s) was not what they pretended to be. It will only make it harder to know what to trust.

This is more of why I said we need to come at it where we ask them to trust their own reasoning, the Bible, and God instead of trusting us. This means you will need to be sure you are challenging them on the things that came from the cult. Try to help them find how to be rid of them, but only them. Nothing of what they believed on their own before that should be attacked. It may be something to discuss later on as you would discuss it with anyone who never was in a cult. But the focus needs to be on what they have not truly thought about before. If it is what they already believed, it is not a part of the brainwashing (unless that was done by someone else).

This is part of how to fight their fear of the outside world. As they realize more of the deception and threats came from inside the cult, they will see more of what the cult claimed to be lies from the outside world were not lies at all.

As they see this, it will do more to help with their trusting of their own minds. We are trying to get them to distinguish between the thoughts they had and the thoughts they were given so they can see all of the fears came from that one place—the cult's brainwashing.

Even more than that, do not—I repeat DO NOT—let yourself try to convince them of what you believe. No matter how true and crucial of a belief it is. That should only be a discussion after you can be certain they are the one accepting it. And it cannot be an attempt to persuade.

As soon as you go down that road, to them you are doing the exact same thing the cult did when they first joined. It is when it can be a *reasonable* discussion that it is worth approaching.

It is when we show we are not putting ourselves as being the one they have to follow that they can start to see we are there as a servant or assistant, not a demanding leader or a luring "friend". This causes them to find we are far different from what their previous community was.

While fighting these fears, the hard part in who they trust comes in helping them distinguish what is truly their own, personal thoughts from what is there as a result of the brainwashing they were put through when they joined the cult. It is this battle with what the cult has buried deep within the darkest corners of their minds that can be one of the most difficult steps.

They will often start doubting themselves and wondering if the leadership was correct. They begin thinking through it toward those thoughts that will stir up those fears they escaped. The teachings down in there will be surrounded by many other implications, persuasions, false memories, and fears.

This would be a good thing to consider on both sides. However, for someone in this situation they will lose the logic necessary for this, because the fear will once again take control of all their emotions and thoughts.

It is necessary for them to have someone with them to pose the questions fear will not direct them to ask. Fear will always skip "Is this true?" and go straight to "What if this is true?" Pointing them toward the first question will help them look at what showed them it was false previously. When they see that, the answer to the second question does not matter.

The questions almost always go this kind of direction. They will differ, but fear will always skip the questions that really matter. It is reasoning that is hard to find when fear gets in the way. Many of the times I try to help someone in a state of complete despair, I have to keep trying to encourage them in their ability to fight it and continue on while, at the same time, knowing they are not considering what I am saying. It can be clear they are unable to truly consider what is being said. However, I have to give them some encouragement for them to think about after the "episode" has calmed down. When questioning it, this problem is likely to be an issue.

My sister was always afraid of sharks. When we were younger, but starting to grow, our parents let us see some parts of "Jaws". After watching it, my sister had constant nightmares.

My parents would try to calm her down. My mom asked, "What's wrong?"

My sister said, "Shark is gonna eat me."

My mom would ask, "Can the shark come out of the ocean?"

"No."

"Can the shark come into the house?"

"No."

"Can the shark come into your room and eat you?"

"No."

With my sister admitting this, my mom asked, "Then what's wrong?"

"Shark is gonna eat me!"

Her fear was so in control of her mind it would not let reasoning get through. This is why the teachings of a cult are explained with the word "brainwashing". Their brain is being cleared of all reasoning so they can fill it with fear and lies so that, even after they have seen the issues and fallacies, it will have little to no affect.

Consider what it can take for a child in this situation to calm down? Sometimes a mother just needs to stay there and watch them fall asleep. They need to be there for them. But, trying to talk and teach them does not bring the correct kind of help by itself. It is encouragement they need most to stand against the fear, and that takes being there as support so they know they have a friend and assistance outside the illusions as well as inside of them.

This is another reason why, even if those dealing with despair weren't listening to me, it was good for me to be there encouraging them. They needed to know there was someone with them and trying to help them. What my statements tried to communicate may not have been heard, but the tone of my voice and the attentiveness they could hear in it was able to communicate what they needed—that I cared and was there for them.

***

It is the way these thoughts and fears keep sneaking in that keep this process from ever completing the goal. There is always something in their memories and thoughts that can cause new doubts and raise more questions. The previous indoctrination is what causes these to push them in the wrong direction with such force, but it can still come even if the indoctrination can be undone.

There are many little things able to help in keeping these thoughts from coming as often. There are ways to make it so that, when they come, they will be unable to do much.

And, once again, what is needed will depend somewhat on the person.

One option to fight these thoughts can be getting as far from the place one has left as possible. It can be helpful in having little around them to bring back the memories of the lies and threats. They will feel like they have truly started a new life and they are even farther from the dangers they fear.

Also, if it is harder for one to go back because of the distance, it can be more of a hinderance. They may start questioning enough that, if they are nearby, they will go back, but if there is a greater distance, it will not be so easily done and give them more time to reason through it. This will also give the push of the doubts time to calm before they are able to return.

In other cases, however, being closer can be what it takes to keep their guard up. For some, when being nearby and keeping an eye on what is happening, they can be constantly reminded of what the cult does, how they work, the pains they cause, and the lies they tell. If close enough, with some cults, they will be likely to see more disdain from the cult, because they are going to be seen as more of a threat if they remain nearby.

They will also see the lives the members are living. They will see the way the members have been brainwashed and made blind that keeps their doubts from growing. However, as I said, for some it may not be good to be near this, but for others, this can be a constant reminder of the leashes the cult had on them.

Some may find they need to avoid any fellowships that may have any similarities to the cult. If it was a large community and they want to keep going to church, they may need to stick to smaller Bible studies. If it was a smaller community, it might be better to find a larger church.

On the other hand, some may need the similarity in where they go. It can be the contrast that will help them. Some may start to see enough similarity to make the comparison and they will notice how where the differences are is in every part that was causing trouble. It will give them more reassurance they made the right choice by abandoning not just the cult, but the false teachings specifically.

This contrast in the needs of different people is another reason they need the support. Finding how to stand strong against it can take seeing what is happening from more than one angle. The more often they have someone to discuss it with and share the secrets with, the better.

This is a major part of getting out of so many different things beyond just a cult. It could be having been in a corrupt business. It could be from being in a dishonest church. Whatever the case, when there are secrets, they need to be let out.

I have been through a couple cases where I have held onto secrets of what really happened in situations because I did not want to gossip. I felt like that would be wrong for me to gossip about these things, so I stayed quiet even when asked about it.

Then, while I was rereading the Bible for myself, I found one assumption I always heard about Adam and Eve was not in the Bible. Every class I'd been in would talk about how they both tried to "shift the blame". First Adam accused Eve, then Eve accused the serpent.

Reading it again, I realized it was an assumption they were basing their accusations of them on. When, in reality, Adam and Eve both confessed what they did and told the whole story. They both would say, "And I ate." I recognized that God never rebuked them for these acts of "gossip", and He practically gave them each a sort of "vengeance" within the curses He put on each of them. Considering this passage in a new way, it started to make me question when we should or should not be pointing out another person's sins or secrets.

Later, on dictionary.com, I found what gossip was defined as: "idle talk or rumor, especially about the personal or private affairs of others." This showed me too many things I kept hidden were not idle talk or rumor. The lies of a religious group, company, etc. have nothing to do with things that are personal and/or private. Anything someone hides to trick or confuse someone else is no longer a personal and private matter. Realizing we have too general of a definition of gossip at times, I found holding back the truth meant I was helping tell the lies. Taking any revealing of a truth that may seem negative as gossip is something too many people are made to do—usually by those who told the lies.

This is often a very effective tool of cults. I cannot tell you how many times I have received a comment on one of my videos rebuking me, because I do not have the authority to judge HH. Almost every single time, when I check who the user is, I find it was a new account created that day just so they could make the comment.

This makes it so they can use that way of thinking to not only silence the members who left, but also those who have not joined. Yet, they are using such hypocrisy in judging of judging. This is what happens when they are truly trying to shift the blame.

When someone comes out of the cult they were in, it can be best for them to share the secrets. By that, I do not mean they need to be proclaiming the secrets as publicly as possible, but they ought to be sharing it to at least one or two other people they trust enough.

This is not just because they need to tell others, but they also need to tell themselves. Originally, they spent a lot of time convincing themselves these things were not the bad actions of a cult, but entirely their own mistakes. As I spoke of, the cult will often put blame on the innocent party to keep them silent about the true errors.

Once out, they need to wash out all of these lies they were told and will keep telling themselves.

It is so difficult, because no matter how many times one cleans out deception, there will always be a couple stains to keep scrubbing.

But can they "fully" escape the doubts? Can they completely be rid of the thoughts the cult buried deep in their minds and keep them from popping back up?

No.

But that is not because they are controlled anymore. It is because no one can. None of us have. No matter where you are in life, no matter what you believe, no matter what your past is, the lies can always be whispered in your ear. This is not because of who you are, nor is it always because you are vulnerable. Sometimes, it can be because you are a threat to the lies.

I was not approached by my previous friends to try and bring me into HH until I started spreading the truth and warning of the lies. They came after me not because they saw me as easy to trick or a good addition to their community. They came because they wanted to stop what I was doing and use me as more proof they're right.

Though it is much harder for them than most, those who leave need to learn this is not just their battle. They were never alone in this fight, and they were not in that position because they are seen as weaker (the cults would love to have the stronger on their side). With everything I have found about HH, I have had to find extra confirmation because my own doubts constantly try to overcome me. It is why it is such a loved tool of the enemy. Sometimes, even when it does not trick us, it can weaken our guard. Those leaving a cult need to learn they are not fighting anything we aren't, and they should not be letting themselves fear them. The liars are not stronger than them—only slyer.

This world is full of lies. The only way to find complete safety from them is in Jesus. He is not of this world. Keeping faith in Him is a guard that can work against anything. The attacks and lies will still come and try to penetrate, but there is one place those who leave a cult can turn to find that safety.

Yet, in a world full of and built upon lies, the escape from it and the deceit's attacks is only complete when the end of this state of the world comes. And that is why we must all constantly keep our guard up. Not as the victims but as the fighters.

Chapter 9:

Gaging the Water's Temp

So many times, I have heard those stories with the line, "I never thought it would happen to me." When I hear it, I usually am surprised people would be so oblivious.

Then my friends joined a cult. Now I understand what that feels like. Having spent so much time looking for information about cults, I also understand why I was so unprepared, and why more need to be warned. It became what drove me this far.

Above all else, I do my videos and write this book to prepare other brothers and sisters for the wolves that will try to penetrate the flock. What happens to those who already joined I have little impact on until they start questioning HH and look into my channel. What the community around HH does about them is not something I have any expectations of. What I can fight for, and is my primary goal, is for the Christian community to be aware of the deception of HH and other cults trying to sneak in.

***

As I have mentioned already, the most unique part of HH I have seen is how they rarely recruit anyone who is not already in Christian churches or communities and their recruiting is done inside these communities. This is something other cults do, but it is not the only method they will use. HH on the other hand avoids other methods as much as they can partly to help in not raising suspicions too easily.

This is what makes them the perfect example of what I feel there is a need to warn of.

Going back to the Bible's warnings of the wolves among the sheep, the problem I have been noticing is how the majority of the churches talk about this with the idea of it being about corrupted people being in the church. They have a focus on those believers who may be stumbling, those leaders who are dishonest or greedy, and anyone who is bringing in some new practices, music, etc.

The guard of most churches is down because the idea of these wolves being able to bring in false teaching is silently assumed to be the least likely kind of wolf to penetrate the church. And the potential of these wolves being a cult taking advantage of, penetrating, or coming out of a church is the one considered least.

Before I started looking at cults, I assumed they were so offtrack and contrary to Scripture they must be drawing in the most lost people. There were examples of cults pulling in people who were going through a lot of difficulty that was making them question a lot about what they believed and what was true. It caused me to assume cults would target primarily those who knew little and were unsure what they believed. Finding out the opposite was true was terrifying.

What they do is try to convince you they are on the same side. They want to make you come to the assumption they are godly, Christian men and women. Then, they can begin to show you bits of where they disagree. After some calm discussions about these things, they can begin to turn the heat up.

One of my very first warnings, from so much I have heard from so many different cults' histories, is to never let someone speak at your church, teach in your Bible study, or lead in any way in prayer groups, unless you are certain you know and are okay with what they believe and teach. This may seem obvious, but they are not going to do this bluntly. They will try to find a more subtle way of doing it.

Also, if a visitor does speak up and something unexpected comes out, do not take it lightly. Make sure they are not letting it go too far in any direction away from the gospel. It is something to be aware of. Blair Adams claimed to often speak at many churches across the country. This is spoken of in different ways, different times, and different places enough that I am confident saying there is truth to it. He also mentioned that he had no particular church he was attending at the time because of all his travels. This I have no reason to doubt. And I have reason to believe it, because this is what I have heard of other cult leaders doing before they had their following.

As you can hear in many stories of the origins of cult leaders, they will go out trying to share their message of what God has "shown" them, or how they have come to "see" Scripture, to different churches or leaders. Many will reject them and get rid of them. This will upset the leaders and, instead of this making them question and reanalyze their teachings, they begin to try starting their own "church" that ends up becoming a cult.

After this has happened to them multiple times at the start, they will know they can't just go in and start showing the "truth" to bring people in. They now understand they need to be more careful, and they know they can't bring the entire church over to their side. It has to be those they can pull in. It will give them some hope of the new followers convincing their friends and family as well, but those sneaking in to the church will want to give as little opportunity as possible for those more cautious to question them.

Sometimes, they may do it as HH often does. A couple leaders will go to the church and act as though they are visiting. Then, they will go to smaller Bible studies or prayer groups. In these smaller gatherings, they will begin to plant these ideas that will be odd but seem innocent at first glance.

This is where they may try to find an opportunity to teach more subtly. In a smaller group, it can feel a little less awkward for them to be sharing their opinion or beliefs. However, they aren't often speaking as though they are only sharing their opinion.

My first personal suggestion is to always be on guard when they immediately say something odd or questionable. If a visitor goes to a smaller gathering and spends most of their time listening and trying to get to know what you teach before they say much, that is more reasonable. You would think those who visit would want to be sure of what the congregation believes before they are sharing much or confident that they want to be a part of it.

The first potential sign of this kind of cult's penetration is when someone visits and immediately is sharing/teaching their own views without knowing the congregation's very well, it can be because they feel they know best and need to make everyone else agree with them. There are some I have seen do this who were not cult members. However, they did become one of the first to join HH.

The cult leaders or members who do this will often try to be particularly pleasant about it. This is the second sign one can take as a warning. When their smiles, tone of voice, stature, and/or volume seem so pleasant it feels out of place in what they are saying, this can be a major red flag.

As with those the cult recruits when they visit the cult, they want to give those in the church being visited the most pleasant impression possible. As mentioned, those who visit HH are excited about how welcoming and loving they were.

One of the first things I would say is to make sure you can tell what their motive is. Are they just trying to be nice, or is this a task? Are they wanting to help you, or are they trying to spoil you?

There is a major difference between someone helping someone else carrying a large bag, and a hotel assistant taking all your luggage up to your room. For one it is out of compassion. For the other, it is their job or obligation.

Also consider how hotel workers will go to the point of carrying every piece of luggage, making your room not just clean, but spotless, and placed in the most decorative positions. When you go to a church and people are friendly, great! When you go to a gathering and people are treating you like royalty, be careful. It means they have an obligation to do so. That can be a sign of legalism or something(s) to hide behind the performance they may be putting on.

Even in the calls I was receiving from friends when they wanted to show me why I was wrong about HH, I could sense the tension in their voice, but it was most awkward because of how they still tried to sound like nothing was wrong—or even wonderful.

At the same time, though I tried to just have a chat about how they were doing, they would push in the direction of trying to discuss why I was wrong. When they were unwilling to talk about anything but my own "errors" the pleasantness of their tone was extremely out of place and clearly nothing authentic.

But they can't go too far.

These phone conversations would always end with something like, "You need to visit so you can experience it." It would be the end of the conversation because it was often their last line of defense. They saw they could not counteract me with what they planned to (which was often everything but their teachings). They would find those were the only things I would use in coming against HH and they did not want to try discussing much of that because of their own doubts deep inside, or they would only be able to recite what they were told and would come to a dead-end when I asked for a complete explanation.

The same pattern is followed when they visit a church. They don't want to convince people of their teachings while they are there. That is not the point. Their main goal is to get people to visit their Waco location if they can, to start reading their books, or listening to what services they do put online. This is the third sign, and the most consistent of HH's tools.

They need them to have that experience so they are drawn in before they hear enough of the teachings.

This will be different for other cults, but it will usually follow the same pattern. They want to get you to visit one of their gatherings (what they do to bring this about can be extreme with certain cults). If they can get you to visit, then they can start showing you more of their teachings, because no one else will be around to point out the issues and they will have more support to stand against any potential opposition. The more they can outnumber you, the better for them.

If they do feel you are more interested and will follow their teachings more easily, they may give you a way to read about or listen to their teachings, but it will be different from how other churches may do so.

HH has a site with the sermons given by Blair Adams, Asi Adams, and other leaders. However, you have to have a username and password to listen to them. Getting a username is not the simple task it is with most sites. You need to tell them who referred you to the site. If you have a good reference and they have confirmation you are someone they can trust they will create your account. Otherwise, you will be unable to listen to the messages.

I had one person come on my channel when I was getting started, and he shared a username and password he got so that I could listen to the messages. I listened to 4 or 5 before they saw what was happening and blocked the account.

When you see any sign of these characteristics or methods in someone visiting your church, question them further. Make sure they are coming out and bluntly sharing what they believe. If there are any doubts, let it out. Don't keep those questions in your mind. If you are wrong about it, they should be able to explain and make things even more comfortable for everyone there. If you are right to be cautious, what they say will either show their errors or avoid the question and only raise your concerns, and hopefully others'.

When you need to do this, do not put it off. Unless you can tell everyone else there is also concerned, talking to others there about it after they have been pulled in may do little good. There needs to be as little time as possible allowed for those deceptive thoughts and comments to seep into the minds of any nearby brothers and sisters.

My second suggestion is particularly for those who lead a Bible study or prayer group. If you find someone like this visits and suggests any of those who join your meetings to visit where they go, do not hesitate to investigate. Immediately do your research. Find out what this congregation teaches and what they do. Do not wait until your members come back from a visit to ask them what they were taught. Find out first so you can show them the issues you are noticing. And you can make sure they understand the important truths they need to keep in mind. If they do insist on visiting, this will hopefully make the issues and falsehoods stick out to them.

My third suggestion is the most difficult one to give, due to how severe it can seem to be.

When someone joins your fellowship, church, prayer group, or gathering, and with any confidence they begin teaching or suggesting any direct falsehoods, do *not* hesitate to eliminate. Confront them immediately. If they cannot explain themselves as possibly erring in their wording or explanation and insist on these teachings being taught, be rid of them. Even if they are not what may be considered a wolf in sheep's clothing, they are an infected sheep. You do not want this infection spreading.

Yes, it can be good to stay in contact with them if you think you can show them what is wrong with what they teach. However, this does not mean you should take the risk with something like this.

There was one man, I will call Thomas, who joined our home church and Bible studies for a little while. The more time we spent with Thomas, the more our concerns grew. We would find him taking passages out of context, sharing passages with his own, odd wording, and teaching things leading the wrong way.

After some of those who led our groups (including Zach)

confronted him, he stopped coming to most of our gatherings. However, one leader, we will call Nick, was the most patient, loving, and thus vulnerable. It is something he has grown stronger in, but it was a lot more of an issue at the time.

Thomas began coming on occasion to what meetings we had at Nick's home, because he knew Nick was the least likely to ask Thomas to leave. Nick would always give him a chance to try and show Thomas love and bring him around.

We had a meeting at Nick's house one night, and Thomas came a bit late. Nick was quick to invite him to join in.

That night, while everyone was sharing prayer requests and praying over different people, I was in the back of the room where it was darker due to photosensitivity—I often have to be cautious of this.

I could see Thomas was standing a little ways off as well, but he began to go through his Bible as though there was something he wanted to share because of what they were praying for.

Being concerned what he would try to promote, I began praying for God to silence Thomas if he was going to try sharing any more of his falsehoods.

After a few short prayers, I looked up to find Thomas was looking at me with an expression of both fear and anger. When I stared at him with a straight face and without backing down, he turned, grabbed his Bible and left before anyone could say anything.

Any false prophet or false teacher will take every chance they can get. We can never let our guard down. And this is not just the guard of our own hearts and minds, but those of our brothers and sisters.

The enemy makes themselves look like what they are not. Satan acts as an angel of light. This is why our guard within the churches needs to be where it is the strongest. Even when those attacks don't come as often, this causes more need for preparation. Those battles we don't fight as often are the ones the enemy knows we are less likely to be ready for.

Another thing that is a little less common but done consistently by HH is their targeting of families.

They want to pull in the families more than they will put effort into drawing in those who are single. It is a clever strategy when you watch how they use it.

After our friends were pulled in, some of us took a look at who they seemed to target and who they seemed to ignore. The most consistent thing we noticed was how they approached the couples who were going to the same gathering.

When someone, such as myself, was single, they would never approach them. When someone, such as one friend, went to a different church or had different beliefs to their spouse, they would not approach them unless they saw a vulnerability. It was those with a spouse who was going to the same gathering they seemed to target.

Another similar characteristic we started noticing was more consistent within those who joined (in and out of our community) than those they targeted. Many of the parents in the family would have come out of a family without, or with a weak, father figure. We started noticing the lack of consistency in the earlier families made them draw them in more, and in some cases, the leadership could end up filling the hole left in the family—even if they did not fit into the hole well, it could seem to be something they always sought deep down.

Watching both how HH would approach previous members and how I saw them approach friends who left, they take this to their advantage by trying to separate anyone who questioned them from their spouse and children (even before they would leave).

If you remember, I mentioned the friend I was calling David, and how he left HH. What I did not speak of was what happened with his family. I am glad to say, when he decided to leave, he called his wife and told her he was leaving. He asked if she would go with him. She agreed and they got their whole family out of HH.

However, part of the reason they would separate David from his family at that point was to make it more likely his wife would look down on him and refuse to leave, or make him more subservient in order to reconnect with his family sooner. They can then take advantage of it as a way of keeping the spouse, who left, silent or pulling them back in later. It would be the only way for them to stay in contact with their family. They temporarily put a collar on them, and how they do gives HH an extra leash in case the member burned their collar.

This is something to be aware of in general. Though other cults may not always target families, there are often certain kinds of people they will pick out. In general, religion would want to pull anyone into the "truth". Cults want those who will make them stronger, or they will have more control of. Some may target students, particularly younger ones who may not know as much yet to be less aware of peculiarities in their teachings. Others may go after people skilled in particular areas where they may be of assistance in goals the cult has to reach. They do often treat it more like a business might treat looking for employees.

When you can see this—when those doing the outreach are specifically talking to certain kinds of people—there is a higher chance you are dealing with a cult. They are not concerned with spreading the truth. They are concerned with recruiting.

One thing that I have to confess even I feel ashamed I did not realize for a while is possibly the most obvious warning.

When you have people come and visit your church, it will usually be for one of four reasons. Frist, they may come because they are on vacation and just wanted to be at a service somewhere that week. Second, they may be visiting family or friends and coming with them. Thirdly, they are moving to the area and looking for a church. Lastly, they are part of a ministry your church supports and are there to share what they are doing.

The fourth category is obviously the one you will have little to worry about unless your church started supporting them carelessly. If it is the third, one thing they will not do, unless they are trying to trick you, is invite you to their church, but even if so, this will not make any sense and be hard to miss the warnings. If it is the second, they might, but it will be doubtful nothing would have already been happening with their family or friends to give warning signs.

The first is when you know there is a chance of this happening. If they come for this reason and invite you to their church, red flags should start going up. The question to ask yourself in this case is why they are inviting. If they are saying this because they would like you to if you are visiting the area, that would be less concerning (though one should always visit another church with some form of caution until they know their teachings). However, if they want you to visit simply because they think you should come to see their church, this should make the flags wave like they are in a hurricane.

If they visit your church and are pleased, they should be following the same teachings, and this would give no reason for them to feel you need to visit somewhere else. If they are pleased with what is happening at your church, why would they feel there is any need for you to consider going to another church? Let alone how they are going even further and suggesting you should visit *their* church despite how far it may be from where you are. What makes theirs the one special from all others across the country?

If there are lessons or teachings they think might help you or encourage you, they should be able to give you a suggestion for a book, or a sermon. They should not be seeing a need for you to come to their particular church. Their focus would be more on the problem.

If they are doing this, there is more than a teaching they feel you need. They feel there is something you are missing and will find if you visit their fellowship. When someone is looking at things this way, it can be the first sign of them being a cult member. They are putting their "church's" leadership and teachings above those of all other churches— thus cult leaders.

Even if the church these people are part of may not be pushing this to a point where it would be considered a cult, its members having this kind of perspective would show it is going too far in that direction or is not teaching the truth enough to prevent it.

In the last sentence that is prior to the final additional notes, the baptismal agreement of HH makes the statement, *"Thank you for your prayerful seriousness in this most serious of matters."* (p. 136) It is this treatment of joining their ministry as the most serious matter that shows they see your choice of a church as not just as important but even more important than your acceptance of the gospel itself.

Always avoid any gathering that members of come to you, say they believe the same things as Christians, say they believe you are saved, and then tell you that you need to come to their gathering. If they truly believe that you need something, they believe you are missing something that is crucial, thus, they don't believe you are fully saved. What they are claiming is a paradox whether or not they recognize it.

Then there are times the cults come to you on the street, at your school, business, etc.

These are times where sharing you are also a believer should be enough. If they start checking what you believe or trying to pull you in further, be aware of how they go about it. There are a few things they may do. Not that they always will, but if they do, it can be a warning.

First of all, if they never ask about what church you attend before suggesting joining theirs or their studies or prayer groups it can be a bad sign. This can come from an assumption they are making that you are in the wrong church even though they do not know what church you are in. This points in that direction of them treating their own community as above the rest.

Maybe they will ask you this in order to make you a little more comfortable. In this case, the second thing to be aware of is if they pay attention to your answer. How do they respond to this church's name?

Are they upset by it?

If so, what is upsetting them? If they ask you questions to point out issues, then, you can approach it as you would with anyone who has different beliefs. If they try to act as though nothing is wrong, be on guard and do not trust them. They are hiding something from you. Something that is obviously of significance. This means that if they are approaching you honestly and see it as the truth, that should make them more concerned about showing you the truth.

Are they pleased by it?

If so, good. This won't be a problem. But if inconsistencies begin coming into their questions and reactions, the first reaction was probably an act. Thus, this is another lie they are hiding and should raise your guard.

Or do they seem to ignore your answer and go on as though it did not matter?

If so, that can be the best time to move on. This means they are not hearing you. They are there to teach you, and they will not hear anything you give them as an answer or try to explain to them. When you can't speak to them, there is no reason to try, whether they are of such a group or not.

If you feel ready and are on guard, you may want to start asking them more questions to find out what they really believe. If you choose to do this, my first suggestion will be to make sure they are trying to answer your questions. If they are in false religions or maybe another denomination, they will be reasonable and trying to answer your questions what they can. However, if they avoid the question and/or give long, stretched out answers, this will make it more of a possibility they are part of a cult or something other than what they claim and know telling you too much too fast will scare you off.

Thirdly, they may start to avoid you as soon as they hear what you believe. For some, they will have been taught to avoid any who may fill their minds with lies. When they run into someone with another belief to possibly try convincing them of, they will get away as fast as they can.

This can seem better, however, it is something like this that is a good warning to be more prepared in the future. If there is a nearby cult or religion that teach their followers that way, it can be good to keep your guard up for when the leaders or more well-trained individuals try to approach you. You would want to look into what the nearby churches or "ministries" teach so you can be prepared for when this may happen.

Following along with what I just mentioned, this is something that can be good to be sure of even before something happens—be aware of any nearby cults or false teachers you may have to deal with if you run into them out on the street.

As mentioned, there are times they may target students, or even teachers, at universities. This is another sly method beyond just seeking the young and less well-versed. In this group, coming after Christians can be easier. It is those who profess to be Christians who will often need a church and not have one in this new location.

If they are from other religions, it will be more likely they have already been directed toward another gathering when they left their former church. However, if they are a general Christian, they are more likely to be looking for a church on their own or not looking for one but more open to joining one. This makes them a much easier target for cults to try and pull in.

Inviting another believer to their fellowship, because you need one while attending the university, can remove most of what would raise suspicions if they did as HH does.

In most situations, I hate judging a fellowship or church by its denomination. However, in this kind of situation, the first thing to do would be to ask them what denomination they are part of. If they don't give one, push for them to give you their foundational beliefs.

Again, if they try to hide the answer, avoid the question, or keep it vague, turn it down until you are told more or keep your guard and analyzation of their teachings high.

Another thing that can happen is someone you know well may join a fellowship and ask you to join.

If this happens, consider if anything about them has changed? If so, what? Is it just their attitude/demeanor, is it for the better or the worse and if it's better, maybe give it a chance. If it is worse, definitely raise your guard. Either way, try to find out what else may have changed.

If the change is more of certain limitations they follow, is it just them, or do they try to push these limits on others? The latter is a warning. If it is the former, then consider how dogmatically they hold to these limitations and if the topic is significant.

The more they are talking about these rules as being crucial, that can be one of the biggest warning signs in this kind of situation.

It would be best to try and warn them even before they try to pull you in, but it can be hard to be sure what is going on until they start wanting to pull you in as well.

Then, there is the importance of being cautious with almost any preacher watched online. Anyone could be wrong in what they teach. Sometimes, it can be to slowly draw you into their teachings.

They will often have an amazing way of wording and teaching things to grab you tighter. Some may use this to sneak in false teachings you would normally be concerned by.

This can happen beyond just occurring within this kind of online, more broadly publicized situation.

There was one couple who joined us when Zach taught. The husband was not crazy about Zach's teachings, but he came because of how much his wife enjoyed them and was enthusiastic about them.

One day, after the service, she was talking about what a great message Zach gave that day. When her husband asked her what it was Zach taught that really got her excited, she was at a loss for words. She realized she could not remember, because it was just his way of speaking and his words that got her, not what he was actually teaching.

This is how the leaders of the cults are able to get these teachings into people's minds without them realizing it. It is something any false teacher can use to get his views into others' minds and get their guards down. They just need to find a way to impress, other than the teachings.

I will say it again and again, "Be on guard!"

It does not matter who you are.

It is those many of us trusted most. Those we saw as the most well taught and versed in the Scriptures HH was able to pull in. What you know, what you were taught, and how much you studied, does not help when they know how to target you. Even the most intelligent people can misunderstand things and make mistakes.

It is about trusting Scripture. It is about trusting God. It is about making sure you never put your faith in men or any man's teachings. It must be in God and His teachings. It needs to be about believing what you believe, not what someone else asks you to sign a contract for that tells you you believe it.

Chapter 10:
Gaining Unattainable Victory

One of my favorite movies is one so many people I know hate. This is because it is exposing what people don't want to see. It is one I personally could not stand my first time viewing it. It is also one of so few examples where I will always be grateful for an explanation the producers forced the filmmakers to add at the end. Otherwise, I would have never realized what it was truly about.

"Seven" is a movie that disturbs as many as it excites. It is about two cops trying to find a serial killer picking his victims based on the seven deadly sins. In this, the characters have many discussions about the city they are in and all the evil in it. They disagree about whether or not it is something they want to keep trying to fix. One character is younger, ignorant, and motivated. The other is older, wiser, and trying to retire to get out of the city. In the final line, the older cop who is the main character, played by Morgan Freeman, decides not to retire and narrates saying, "Ernest Hemingway once wrote, 'The world is a fine place and worth fighting for.' … I agree with the second part."

When I stopped to consider this after my second viewing, I could not deny the truth of it. This world is filled with so much deceit and corruption, we cannot expect to fix the issues, but we still need to fight.

Ironically, at the same time as this film alerted me to this, it also made the idea of the seven deadly sins something that keeps disturbing me more and more as I look at the lies and tricks of the cults across our country and the world.

When this list will include things like sloth, gluttony, lust, and envy, how is it leaving out the one that is the very sin Satan used to bring the original fall—deception. Not being in Scripture, I cannot help but fear this list was that very thing—Satan's deception.

One of the most daunting reminders to pray for my friends to leave HH is knowing the history of Waco.

To summarize it quickly, Waco is already known for being where the Branch Davidian cult was destroyed not long from when HH seems to have moved there. The members led by David Koresh died during an unexpected fire started while the FBI held them on siege…rumored to have been by a mass suicide.

What makes this so daunting is the question of what it would take to bring a cult to an end. And yet, no matter what is done and what is shown, some who joined it will refuse to admit the cult's leader(s) was wrong in their claims. The only way it could truly come to an end is by an extreme case of what has come to be called "drinking the Kool-

Aid".

I've heard some ridicule the way this term is used. But anything can become slang and start sounding hollow. For those who know what happened, I personally feel it can be a great reminder. These cults are offering a drink to you they claim is the living water. However, there is a poison in it that will play with your mind and bring another (worse) form of death in a way similar to when Satan convinced Eve to eat the fruit.

Coming against these places can bring a disaster if it is approached in the wrong way.

This is why, before I go into the concept of bringing an end to the lies, I need to make a reminder to, in a sense, "hope for the best and plan for the worst."

It is the impossibility of solving the problem that can become upsetting, depressing, or bring to a point of despair. It is why I keep reminding myself, more than anything, of how there has already been some success. I have already been able to warn a few when HH tried to trick them, a few members (current and former) sent their thanks, and I have been able to help a couple people leaving HH. This needs to be enough. Getting to that point of trying to force an end where it can't be done brings disaster.

It is why this needs to constantly be seen as, not just a fight against the lies, but also, a rescue mission to get those we can out of the building before it is burned to the ground.

***

Just as when getting someone out of a cult, one of the most important words to keep in mind when trying to expose one and find a way to bring it down is "patience".

It is a long process, and it is something that you cannot simply choose to do. Getting people out and preventing people from entering can be a starting point, but it is not until the right people come out and the right timing and method is used that the lies can be exposed and brought to their end, or weakened.

When someone leaves a cult, part of the question is how much they know and what they know. Is there anything that can prove the cult leaders are deceiving the people? Is there any proof they are taking advantage of the authority they have gained? Is there anything incriminating of the leadership? If so, that is still a minor step forward.

The most difficult part of this is often finding those who will speak up and finding enough of them.

It can be prevented most easily by what was the difficulty for us for too long. Those who leave or turn against it can always be made to feel like the minority. When one sees the issues of a cult and what is going on under the surface, it can be hard to believe people have not already seen this. With nothing happening one feels alone.

As with some of my friends and myself, we thought we lost all our friends and it was not until we started to speak up that we found the support often needed to encourage people to speak up. It will create its own catch-22 only broken when someone or some people are ready to speak up despite what attacks may come.

For me, it was also difficult because of fear I could have been misunderstanding things they were teaching. However, it was when I asked for clarification while making my videos that those who came against what I was doing only confirmed my concerns.

Once some are willing to question it and raise concerns, there still has to be those from inside who can confirm them.

Most continue living in that state of fear and won't speak up. It is tough, because the last thing one should do is get in the way of the healing of those who leave. That will ruin the purpose of seeking to expose them—freeing those captured.

It is not always a must to have those from inside exposing them, but if one really wants to weaken the cult it can take breaking a leg of one or all of the wolves leading it. This is done best by exposing something illegal or extremely immoral and hidden actions. To make that concrete takes the right witnesses. Those are often the ones deepest in the cult. Those that deep into the cult can be the ones most silenced.

Again, this makes pushing for it go against the whole purpose of trying to expose them.

Ultimately, this makes it helping those who leave and start to be deceived first and foremost in the priorities. It is the rescue missions of those being helped in getting out that will help in several ways.

It is by trying to clear the minds of those who come out, we can obtain more information on what is going on inside. It is how we can be more prepared and well positioned for further rescue attempts. It will slowly help build both our guard and our strategies.

Hearing more of what pulled different people into the cult can help us raise the defenses of those they may try brainwashing later. It is also by learning more of what the cult showed these people to lure them in that can help us see what they were hiding or avoiding. As we learn more of this it can show us more of what we need to target while seeking to expose the cult.

We will also want to find out what is keeping people in. What made those who leave hesitant? What were the methods used by the cult leadership to keep them under their thumb? It can let us know more of what we need to tell those we seek to pull out first. We will have a better idea of how to approach the brainwashing they need to be cleansed of.

Continuing from this, what pushed them over the line? What was it that drove the former member to the point of getting out? Was it something they learned, or something that was done to them? It is this that can offer more ways of waking up those still under the cult's control.

Of course, this is often tricky to use. One has to be careful to only say or do enough to potentially point their thoughts in that direction. As said before, they often need to find the issues and conclusions for themselves. We can only hope to get them to contemplate it.

The last thing happens less often, but when it does, it is the most helpful. It is important to listen for anything that gives more potential of exposing errors of the leadership able to bring them down. It can take multiple people who know about it to get enough information.

Sadly, there are still times one may find the leadership is too good at hiding their errors. This is where being on the aggressive is useful even if it is not being expected to pull out those who have been deceived.

I will never cease being extremely grateful to those I have had share information with me, and some I have met who became friends of much encouragement. They have shown me I was not alone. They gave me more details I would not have had otherwise. They would let me know what I was doing was getting out there and making a difference. However, the majority of my gratitude has to go first and foremost to HH itself.

As I have been putting out more videos about what they teach, they have appeared to counteract it. What they put up was way too in sync with some of what I was trying to expose. What was so great about this is that the more they talk about what they believe, the harder it can be for them to keep it in the façade they gave it. They gave me further confirmation each time they would attempt to counteract what I spoke up against.

By coming out and fighting more, they are also exposing

themselves further.

There is one thing to keep in mind if you see a place that seems to be deceiving people like this and want to expose them. Do not worry about them accusing you. Don't let anything they do to try and make you look bad bother you or change your focus. Whether or not you have the issues will not matter. You should not be the one people are trying to follow. This needs to be about people trying to follow the truth. The cult leaders are the ones trying to lead and control people. What they are going to accuse you of makes no difference in what they are doing and whether or not it is wrong.

Their primary goal in this is to change the focus to being on suspicions of you instead of them. If you ignore what they are saying and continue focusing on what they have wrong, it will be useless to them to continue.

It is something I had to learn while doing my YouTube channel.

I was having multiple comments accusing me of things, and still have some from time to time. Previously, I would, at times, say things on certain videos to clear things up. I realized it was pointless, and I just focused on the issues in HH.

Over time, these accusations came less often. When they came, I would give short responses within the comments exposing what they were trying to do and/or the hypocrisy of what they were saying. This kept what they were doing from having the effect they were hoping for.

Once you approach it more this way, those who notice it will see their errors, or they will have no way of being able to come after you with it. It will only make things worse for them.

I have had one commentor in particular who has come at me with many essay-length comments on most of my videos. However, I have never had any reason to speak up, block his reactions, or even comment on his comments. Everything he would say only helped.

His reasoning had no logic behind it. Many of his statements were gibberish, and his own views were so far out there no one with any reason to accept HH would listen to them. Everything he said only helped, because it showed how many of those standing strongest against me were not being reasonable.

There is no reason to try and defend against an opponent who is stabbing themselves and your other opponents.

Our focus needs to stay on fighting against the lies, in defense of those they try to deceive, and to rescue those already tricked.

As I explained earlier, when I started attempting to spread awareness and explanation of what HH is, I did not want to. I had found cults interesting when I heard about them, but they were never something I looked into. I looked into HH because of my concern for my friends. I dug further because of how little I could find.

This is where the real fight on the offensive comes in. It is both aggressive and passive at once.

Fighting against and exposing a cult is not done the way trying to evangelize can be done. Going out and talking to random people on the street is going to do little, and nothing if you are not located near this cult.

This is one of the blessings that comes with the internet.

It is having information out there in a place like that which can be most effective at starting to prepare. When people in a cult start to question it, or those being reached out to by a cult have concerns, there needs to be more for them to find online than just what the cult has put up as its teachings. More people who learn of these places need to speak up. Not to everyone they can, nor does everyone who knows have to, but enough need to in places where those who have questions can find it.

When one goes searching for information regarding HH on YouTube, there are generally three things that will come up: the videos of HH, videos of people who visited recreationally, and mine. It was how previously it was the first two only—unless one dug deep enough— that drove me to do what I did. I could tell there needed to be something there for those who heard about HH and were curious or concerned.

This is aggressive in how I have to stand against the accusations and brainwashing of those who come against my videos. It is passive in how I have to wait for those who need to see it to choose to view it on their own.

This can be done also by what I am doing now in writing a book, or books. It can be through putting articles or blogs up (as has been done by the few former members who do speak up). It could be through what is currently starting to be attempted—taking the cult to court.

This last one is the big one and the most difficult.

It is when an opportunity to take things to court shows itself that things can begin to bring those sparks of hope. It can be a long process the cult will make drag as slowly as possible, but if there are any grounds and one pushes through it, it can be what will start to make word spread enough to make that difference.

It is one thing I cannot personally give much advice on, nor am I able to do anything with this myself. However, I can say this is the best place to make a huge dent in their façade.

At the same time, there is that concern of Waco's history and the disasters of other cults that can start eating away at the back of my mind. What would lead to another fiasco?

When considering this, it is important to keep reminding myself how, even if it comes to that, being cautious can make me certain it would only be due to how the leaders respond to their fear of losing control. If nothing is done, those tricked will stay in the deceit. If it is fought, some can come out.

I realized, even if it can cause the leaders of that cult to go too far it is something in their own approach and views causing it, not the way others go about opposing them. It will be happening eventually if they are left to continue doing what they do. Letting this concern silence you lets them have more control via fear.

***

There is one suggestion I have no matter what your approach or how much you hope to do. If you want to do anything to counteract the cult, don't do it alone.

This is for two reasons.

First, don't go without support. At the start I was glad to have a couple friends who had a similar view of it, but it was not until I was about 6 months through that I had others fighting as I was. It made a huge difference.

The pressure of doing it alone was getting to be too much at times. My own worries and doubts would keep me nervous and make me question myself. If I did not find others giving the extra affirmation, I don't know if the stress would have been too much.

More importantly, having only one perspective makes it so you will miss some things. Having someone else with you in the struggle will let you get a more complete image of what they are doing and the approaches both you and those opposing you can take. It will keep your guard up, and make you more able to catch what they may do in response.

It was having those from inside HH and others looking into it while I did that helped me see more than just the lies of what they taught. My focus was so much on those things, I would not have realized the repercussions of what they were teaching if I did not have others sharing information from the other side of the coin.

This is crucial when trying to expose them because it will bring more evidence of what they are doing and make it harder for those in denial to ignore. Every piece of confirmation will help both in your convincing of those in the lies and your own strength in your confidence of what you are standing up for.

This is why reading Blair Adams's books was not enough. I needed to hear the sermons. I had to hear the testimonies of former members. I had to hear the stories of those who visited HH.

Getting a full picture gives those who oppose it more reason to stand firm.

It is also important to have others because of how many different ways of standing/fighting against them there are.

Everything being discussed in this chapter can be too much for one person. Each one is too much effort to handle all of them. But they are also so different in what they take and the kind of challenge they are that it would be best to have people of different skills opposing it.

Some can be more centered around trying to reach those inside the cult and trying to help them get out. It can be important for them to watch more of what is happening within the community itself. They will want to know what is currently happening that can potentially open the eyes of the members.

It is good to see, when some leave, what got them to that point. It can help in learning about changes that may happen within the cult.

This is also where a lot more stress emotionally will come into the task. A task such as this is most difficult for those more unguarded and/or weaker emotionally. You need to be ready for this, but it is rewarding.

Beyond just getting people out, it will bring more clarification what the significant issues are to the more social side of the cult.

This reaching of those inside is personally what I would be most eager to do. However, with my condition, it is not as open of an option. This is why I remain doing what I do and why I believe it is what God wants. Finding one's task takes that leading.

What He pushed me toward is to be finding and exposing their teachings and practices. This can be the most disturbing part to face. You will be looking into how the brainwashing works and seeing some of the evilest parts of what is being done in the leadership of the cult. But what will prepare you for this can come from experience that does more training than any lessons could.

I can now say I am grateful for a struggle I had when I was younger. I used to fight my temper constantly. The battling of this gave me the patience I have now. If I saw what I've been seeing now while still struggling with my temper, I can't imagine how many patches would be in my room's walls by now. Having the calm and beneficial conversations I've had with those opposing me would never have happened. I would have been a mess.

There is certainly a time the teachings and practices go far enough it is a time for anger. But having control of one's anger is also important for looking into these things, and keeping a level head, to be certain you are looking at it logically enough and only letting the final conclusions have influence on your reactions.

One task that rationally comes alongside this is the preparing and warning of others who may oppose or have to face the lies of the cult. It is knowing what they teach and what is between the lines that will help others be on the defensive. They need to be able to spot the false teachings.

Getting word out to the communities the cult is targeting is what has been difficult. I have been thrilled to see there are some who grow concerned by what HH does to penetrate a church. They are some of those who will find my videos and be more able to stand against HH. It is enabling them that has been most rewarding in this. However, it also disturbs me how many have not heard or looked into it. It is spreading word to those who would not look into it on their own that remains the greatest challenge.

This can be assisted by some with another task.

It is also important to know how the cult operates behind the scenes. Those looking into their methods of operation and the social side of how they operate can do a lot in helping people to know what will be used to trick them and how people are held onto.

I am more grateful for the information I get from the former members opposed to HH than almost any other details I've received. It is the comparison and contrast between their practices and their teachings that help me to see what beliefs they truly hold to and put to use. It helps me find which ones are only there for their image.

This also leads to a task some of those doing this will take up, but it also can be the most stressing. That is when exposing the immoral and/or illegal sides of their operations will become the focus.

It is this task often requiring those who are the most specialized, talented, and educated in particular areas. Knowing the rules and laws broken by a cult will be of little use unless you know, or find someone who does know, enough about how the laws work.

This is the side of it I am least fit for. I have less I can say about it, but I will say this is what they will keep most hidden. You need to be ready to truly dig and fight for the information. It has made those starting to come at HH from this angle the most encouraging for me.

This can assist those trying to warn potential targets. Things like this can help spread word faster than the other ways of opposing a cult. It is by this people will start looking into what this place teaches.

This is why it is best when everyone doing these tasks is able to help one another. By knowing what is happening on this side of the coin, I can be focused on what I need to watch for and be able to help spread word on it further. It will also help me by showing what sides of the cult need to be exposed more to answer questions people will have.

Just as each of these tasks work together, there is another task everyone needs to be ready to take on to some extent. Everyone has to be ready to assist, encourage, and stand up for those who come out of a cult.

It is a task needed to be taken on by all family members, friends, colleagues, etc. Some to more extents than others, but these people have faced the most constant form of indoctrination you can imagine. Having support there able to help no matter where they are is important.

Some may be going beyond just being ready to help and encourage when needed. It is something everyone needs, but those from a cult need discipleship stronger than others. Discipling them can be crucial if they are going to be kept from being drawn back toward the lies they were indoctrinated with. It's the battle being fought even if the war is won.

We need to fight for the truth, and it is a war…"not against flesh and blood."

With everything that is done to oppose places like this, always remember weakening it, or even taking it down, is useless if you are not ready to help those inside when they come out.

Fighting a cult is worth doing only because it can help and free those trapped in their indoctrination. Coming at it solely with hate and too aggressively will defeat the purpose. It will make those still inside the teachings of the cult unwilling to hear you.

As I have to remind commentators on my videos constantly, I am fighting against the teachings and where it leads, not the members. We need to be fighting for them.

Chapter 11:

Previews of What's to Come

Here I want to talk about something some may feel is almost off topic, but I will be showing more of HH's false teaching as well. However, I am writing this because I have found there is something to be learned or understood better from looking at cults that can be beneficial even if one never has to deal with the influence of one.

While all of this was happening, the Bible studies I was a part of were doing a lot of studying of Revelation. We were reading it again for ourselves to try coming at it from another angle. We were trying to look at it with an open mind and trying to be prepared to see it when it happens instead of trying to predict it before it did.

However, what I saw it did show more of looked too familiar at times.

The false prophet and the beast are often focused on when a movie, tv series, or book series tries to create a portrayal of the end times. They are major parts of what happens. Many find them intriguing and consider who they may be.

My most recent look at them, my focus shifted. I saw these men will be leading both religiously and governmentally. Everyone had to have a mark of the beast to follow this single leader. The people saw him as their savior.

I felt I was reading about a global cult.

> …the whole earth marveled as they followed the beast. And they worshiped the dragon, for he had given his authority to the beast, and they worshiped the beast, saying, "Who is like the beast, and who can fight against it?"
> And the beast was given a mouth uttering haughty and blasphemous words, and it was allowed to exercise authority for forty-two months. It opened its mouth to utter blasphemies against God, blaspheming his name and his dwelling, that is, those who dwell in heaven. Also it was allowed to make war on the saints and to conquer them. And authority was given it over every tribe and people and language and nation, and all who dwell on earth will worship it, everyone whose name has not been written before the foundation of the world in the book of life…
> - Revelation 13:3-8 (ESV)

This is the model followed by most cults. A leader comes as though bringing the message of God—though actually the lies of Satan—and takes authority to distort the truth and make people believe the beliefs of true Christians are false.

> Then I saw another beast rising out of the earth. It had two horns like a lamb and it spoke like a dragon. It exercises all the authority of the first beast in its presence, and makes the earth

and its inhabitants worship the first beast, whose mortal wound was healed. It performs great signs, even making fire come down from heaven to earth in front of people, and by the signs that it is allowed to work in the presence of the beast it deceives those who dwell on earth, telling them to make an image for the beast that was wounded by the sword and yet lived.
-    Revelation 13:11-14 (ESV)

One story I have heard told similarly by two different sources is about what happened during a service at HH when Blair Adams was speaking.

If one listens to recordings of the services at HH—particularly the less public ones—one thing they will hear constantly is the word "amen". Both by the speaker and by the congregation. It is so constant, it becomes void. It is said at times they say some things that have nothing to them. It is treated as though it is some kind of exercise.

During this particular service, people were having trouble staying focused on the message Blair was giving. Unlike the usual services people were not giving their regular "Amen!"

Blair lost his cool. He began lecturing them about ignoring what he was being given by God. After some shouting, he stomped out. One of the leaders went up on stage and began leading the people to weep and repent for what they had done.

This story made me think of this passage from Revelation 13.

To be clear, I am not in any way saying Blair is the final antichrist, but he was an antichrist.

> By this you know the Spirit of God: every spirit that confesses that Jesus Christ has come in the flesh is from God, and every spirit that does not confess Jesus is not from God. This is the spirit of the antichrist, which you heard was coming and now is in the world already.
>
> -   1 John 4:2-3 (ESV)

This is what can be seen as a more common denominator in cult leaders. They are seeking the same thing as the beast will be pursuing.

This passage in I John is one where Blair picked out a very specific translation that took me some time to find to learn what he was doing. In *Is the Church Christ on Earth?* Blair said,

> John affirmed this in his second epistle—declaring there that Jesus is still coming in our human nature (see 2 John 7 Wms.— the ESV fails, typically we're sorry to say, to translate properly the perfect participle of I John 4:2 or the present participle of 2 John 7, and it then adds words to the Greek text, all of which obscures the meaning of both I John 4:2 and 2 John 7). (p.10)

When I read this, two things immediately made me doubt what was being said. First, there is no explanation of what words were wrong and what was wrong in what it would change. Second, Blair says to go to the Wms. which I never used before this. I never saw a reference like this anywhere else. And I have yet to see it mentioned again. So, why did these particular verses require this particular translation?

In my first look at the other translations, I did not see the difference that made Blair come against the ESV. It took some time before I even had a suspicion what he was trying to do by drawing away from that translation.

After finding from my uncle, who is a pastor, that the Wms. is what is called the Williams New Testament, I got a copy to find out what it says differently—particularly in I John 4. Here are both versions:

> By this you know the Spirit of God: every spirit that confesses that Jesus Christ has come in the flesh is from God…
> -   1 John 4:2 (ESV)

> In this way you can recognize the Spirit of God: Every spiritual utterance which owns that Jesus Christ has come in human form comes from God…
> -   I John 4:2 (Wms.)

The real difference is clearly not in what Blair pointed toward. It is in how it says, the words "spiritual utterance" and "human form" instead of "spirit that confesses" and "the flesh". However, if you compare the ESV with other commonly used translations, it is revealing. There is no difference whatsoever with the NASB in this verse. The main difference with the NIV is that it uses "acknowledges" instead of "confesses". (No real change.) The NKJV and KJV, which are the two I have been told HH uses most often, says "of God" instead of "from God."

Seeing this idea of being "of God" and in "human form" have ways of including the teachings of HH if one takes the words differently. They like "of God" because that is what they see themselves as—a part *of* Him. But Blair was pushing for the Wms. to be looked at because he wanted you to see Him not as truly a man but as though he took "human form" for a time.

Here are the versions of the other passage:

For many deceivers have gone out into the world, those who do not confess the coming of Jesus Christ in the flesh. Such a one is the deceiver and the antichrist.
- 2 John 7 (ESV)

For many imposters have gone out into the world, men who do not own that Jesus Christ continues to come in human form. A person like this is the imposter and the Antichrist.
- 2 John 7 (Wms.)

Once again "human form." Also, they like the tense better in Wms. It is not exactly a different tense, but it can be taken as a different tense. They do not like the ESV, because it is not as easy to make it fit what they want it to say. You can still take the tense of ESV the same way as the tense in the Wms. However, this is not as easily done in the ESV. It does not change the meaning significantly, but they are not trying to convince—they are trying to brainwash.

Though the tense is what Blair focuses on, I have found what they really like about the Wms. is that it not only says He took human form, but that He "continues" in it. Again, this will not change how I view it, but it does give them a way to push their false teaching of the Body fully being Christ.

But notice, this is specifically about the antichrist! I see two other things about this HH would prefer. One, the "Antichrist" is capitalized, so they can say it has to be solely about *the* antichrist of Revelation. Secondly, they can claim Blair was not an "imposter" of Christ, but they have less to fight back with on him as a "deceiver".

This shows that under the surface, even Blair Adams himself saw this similarity he had with an antichrist and refused to allow anyone to apply it to him.

When an antichrist such as Blair can hide himself from Christians, it is much easier to comprehend how the beast will be able to deceive the majority of the world.

There is one commonality between so many cults that has been leaping out at me again and again.

So many cult leaders claim to know of the coming of the end. They often give a date for when it will happen. To be honest, I am weary of any speaker or teacher who wants to claim they know much of how it will happen. Yes, if they claim they know when it will happen, that is the biggest warning to avoid listening to them. However, the cult leaders often go to the extreme of knowing exactly the how, when, who, where, and/or what of multiple parts of it—not just the when of its start.

HH does not do this the way some cults do. As always what they twist is done as subtly as possible. But the rest of their teachings does twist the most important part. Their teachings make it so HH is the only protection from the end. They are the community all believers should rely on, because they are following the Lord's will in a way the others are not. It is the common denominator of Cults' teachings on the end.

One thing I did hear twisted significantly, during one of their conferences, was how the speaker treated the passages saying we won't know the hour. He treated it as though it meant too many believers may not know the hour. (Ironically, I could see and hear a bit of nervousness in what was being said in this.)

Though he did not try predicting a date, the way he said it opened the door. He seemed to want there to be a chance some could know the hour, but most who try to predict it will be wrong. This is a pattern I notice often. Their public teachings will walk you up to the line, but they won't take you across it until no one else is watching. Their private teachings are when they will start trying to take the next step because they will be speaking only to those who will go along with it. Though I have yet to see or hear anything of them teaching a specific time, their opening of that door is enough to raise those flags.

This is what we need to be ready for. Even the beast may slowly warm the pot before he steps forward and initiates the boiling point.

The biggest issue I have with the things HH promotes in their end times teachings, alongside their teaching of the gospel, is how they will be the ones there to rescue the world. They do this with as innocent of a sound as possible by implying more than saying.

This is one commonality of some cults. To churches, Christ is our Savior. He is the one who will rescue us at the end. However, these particular cults make themselves the savior God is using—whether before or after it starts.

This is much like what is often seen as likely of the beast. The world will come to him probably because of him bringing peace at a terrible time. It is the union he will bring. That is what these cults teach they will bring or are—thus they often claim to bring the millennium.

HH follows this. As always, they put it as carefully as possible to make it hard to fully understand what they are saying. They will add their own title for their view despite its commonalities with other views. They often claim to have their own "correct" way of seeing that is unique from all others.

Near the end of one of the messages during the 2022 Exodus Conference, it was said by Evan Birdsong,

> What the Lord is really preparing us for, and laying out here, is a realized millennium where the kingdom of God is at hand, and the Spirit filled army of Christ reigns with Him on the earth against our spiritual enemies *now*.

They are claiming they are already reigning with Him. (And yes, he did emphasize "now" when he spoke.)

This does appear to be inconsistent with other things said in this same message, but that is likely because it is a message shared publicly online. They have to be much more cautious.

They use their teachings of the end times to make themselves the deliverance. This makes sense, if logically following their teachings. They are Christ…they are His return.

When I see these cults treating it as though it is the end, and they are the solution for the world, I see nothing but a foreshadowing of what is to come in the time of the beast.

Some may feel there is nothing to worry about. There is no way a cult will draw them in. Maybe, there is no cult anywhere near them. Whatever may make someone certain it is not something they need to be concerned with, I still think believers need to be aware and on guard even if they don't look at it closely.

Not because I am sure they will be pulled into a cult, but I know similar methods will be used on everyone when the time comes or even when any particular leader seeks more control than they should.

One of the more common ways of getting a point across is to use an extreme example. I keep finding these methods of cults are a good warning, because they are extreme examples of many different forms of deception. However, there are other cults hiding better behind the assumptions of what a cult looks like. The beast will be extreme, yet he will hide between many false assumptions.

I often hear people bring up the concept of finding a counterfeit dollar bill by studying the authentic examples enough to be able to quickly spot the differences. They use this to push how studying Scripture and the truth is much more important than studying a fraud. I will agree with this.

However, what I fear too many forget is that you have to study the frauds extremely close to find the smaller differences. If what you are looking at is authentic, you would want to study it more closely. If you are holding a fraud, why not study until finding as many of the flaws as possible? You will see more of what looks authentic as well as the errors. Is that not a good thing that you studied it closely enough to see them? It can also make you more alert to notice some of the more easily missed issues. I am still looking at HH's teachings to make sure nothing snuck through unnoticed.

Every Christian will agree there is a great deal of deception in the world. Many different forms of frauds are out there. Taking a look at how people can fall for something so extreme can be a good warning of what the world may use in a more subtle way to try and trick you.

If we are going to ignore what has deceived fellow believers before, when are we going to be willing to see it when something does make an attempt to deceive us, no matter how severe it is?

Chapter 12:
Never Stop Asking *Why*

"…man looks on the outward appearance, but the Lord looks on the heart," (I Sam. 16:7 ESV) is one of the most often quoted passages. But I did not recognize where it was in Scripture, and what was being talked about, the many times I used to quote it myself. Though the context does not change the meaning in this case, I find it does add a lot more weight to the application of it in certain situations.

This is said to Samuel when God was showing him how He planned for David to be the next king. This was being said while looking for a leader. The outward appearance is what gives leaders extra power. With cult leaders, this is their primary source of power.

Particularly in the case of cult leaders, it is not because of their attractiveness or massive build, but because they appear to be righteous, kind, wise, intelligent, loving, etc. People need to be willing to consider what is in their heart instead of letting the appearances predetermine how they view not just them, but particularly their leadership. They may take this passage and try not to judge this leader based on appearance, but they will let the way he appears lead to predetermining their judgment of his leadership.

But there is a question to ask before trying to apply this passage properly.

How do we find what is in the heart?

It is what is behind our choices that reveals what is in the heart. It is what is driving us. It is our motivation. It is about that one question people get frustrated by most often and many will ask carelessly... Why?

Sometimes, kids ask it constantly for no real reason, it has just become a habit for them. However, it bothers me how there are those times the children ask it because they really want to understand more of what is happening, and the adults refuse to answer as though it is immature to ask.

When kids want to understand things that is a good thing for them to try to do. It is good for them to hear various responses to these questions so they can think through it and start figuring things out.

There are many questions cults don't like. "Why?" is the one they despise. They want your only motivation to be to follow their standards...to obey their rules. You need to trust the wisdom of the leaders instead of following Solomon's example by seeking for God to give you wisdom yourself.

Asking questions is not wrong. God looks at the heart. So, look at the heart and consider, *Why is the question being asked?*

This is the question always good to pose, if one is trying to understand things better. Other times it is posed to challenge. Are you challenging solely out of rebellion, or are you challenging to be certain things are being approached properly. As when a child asks it, one why often leads to another why, and that can be a good thing—as long as it is not asked to a point where one is not using reasoning any longer while hearing the answers to it.

The reason I find this is important to consider is because it is something the world hates right now—it's hated in cults particularly. Until we are posing that question, we are not looking at the part God looks at. With everything we've talked about, it can be seen time and time again how HH and other cults frown on asking questions like these. Their baptismal agreement is all about bringing you to a point where you have no room to ask why, after signing it.

We need to have our guard up if we are going to fight this well.

> "Judge not, that you be not judged. For with the judgment you pronounce you will be judged, and with the measure you use it will be measured to you. Why do you see the speck that is in your brother's eye, but do not notice the log that is in your own eye? Or how can you say to your brother, 'Let me take the speck out of your eye,' when there is the log in your own eye? You hypocrite, first take the log out of your own eye, and then you will see clearly to take the speck out of your brother's eye."
> -   Matthew 7:1-5 (ESV)

This is about rebuking others, but the idea and wisdom behind it can be applied here as well. If we are going to help others being pulled in by cults or already in cults, we need to first be certain we have our own guards up. Knowing all about cults and how to help those coming from a cult is useless if you are not able to defend yourself from the lies that may try to sneak in. The why question is one of the first lines of defense.

As I have mentioned, I constantly find I will start questioning my own conclusions (even in this book I still do). It is by looking at things again and asking the why questions that I keep from being convinced I was wrong about HH.

Our own guard needs to be strong if we are going to accomplish anything in this battle.

Once you are posing the questions to look at the heart of the leader(s), the first question to ask yourself is what is leading the leader(s). Why are they doing what they are doing?

The leader of a cult often wants power. Sometimes they want popularity. But the big question is in the motive of those who honestly believe what they are teaching. If they feel this is the truth and their concern is for people to come to the truth, why would they want to be so sectioned off from the rest of the world? Their first priority is keeping their community within the framework they have set in place. This happens most often because they want to "protect" those following them from being pulled away by the "false teachers". This means they believe they are the ones who know the truth, and everyone who disagrees with them is an enemy of the truth. They are the ones who know best. It comes down to one thing—pride.

With every line of reasoning that can be used by cult leaders, there is at least one of two motives in the drive for what they are doing. They will either be acting out of pride and/or self-centeredness. I have to say there could be exceptions (because I can never be 100% sure), but this is the first thing to watch for and I have my doubts there will be a complete exception.

In the case of Homestead, even though they would say they are separating from the world, they won't admit that it is proud to assume they are the ones who can do it in a way that will fix all the problems. So, keep asking, "Is there anything in how they lead coming from their own desires or arrogance?"

If you see this, they are not even trying to be a shepherd. They are not doing it out of true care for the sheep. They are caring for their own ego.

When there is not one single leader, or there is a group of leaders along side the primary leader, there is more to it. If there is a group of leaders, it can take identifying whose opinions/preferences carry the most weight to know who is truly leading (at least who is leading in the wrong direction). Then, it is not so easy to identify the motives when multiple leaders are getting behind it.

In HH, there are differing opinions from various contacts I have regarding who is the real issue. I personally have my suspicions, but I would need extra confirmation to point at anyone in particular. But it is always through the "why" that we can get a better idea where the problem is coming from.

Finding the why is tricky, because it is not a question of why things are this way or why a rule is in place. Instead, the question is why was this idea posed and why is it being pushed this far. The false motives can be within any of the stages when there are multiple leaders involved. Remember, "This persuasion is not from him who calls you. A little leaven leavens the whole lump." (Galatians 5:8-9 ESV)

It is good to always question any leadership of every church, because no one, or group, will have teaching that reaches the inerrancy of Scripture. If we ever come to a point of avoiding doubting as though it is wrong, or we feel guilt in questioning a church leadership, we are beginning to lift them up to the position of being worshipped.

If you ever fear questioning a leader(s), question where that fear is coming from. Is it something you were taught? Is it something of your own doubts? Is it something that's happened with previous questions?

You may be in a position I've been in for too long: where you are not trusting your own reasoning enough to even question. That can be good, if it is a lack of trusting your wisdom and reasoning. We need to do as Solomon and seek wisdom from Him. However, if it is a lack of trusting yourself, there is an issue. If you can't trust yourself enough to ask questions, it is because you are against your self. We need to put faith in God. He made us individuals, and our new self, when born again, will reveal what that individual was supposed to be. In Revelation, He speaks of giving each their own name that only them and God will know. As talked about in I Corinthians 12, we are each made unique for a reason, we each are made a part of the body individually, and we are each gifted individually. If we are not going to trust our selves, after He has changed us, enough to even pose questions, we are not trusting how God will speak to us and/or may use us. We need to oppose what the sin nature does to us and tells us, but we need to trust we can take the tasks we are given by Him.

Questions are seeking answers. Trust is at its minimum when questioning. It is when you no longer feel a need to question that your trust in your own wisdom and reasoning is where it shouldn't be.

At the same time… If you cannot ask questions, are you truly believing it? Or are you trusting another's beliefs instead of deciding what you believe? Have you received your answers from men or from God? Even God has answered those who have asked Him questions. When the disciples asked Jesus questions, He did not rebuke them for questioning Him. His harsh rebuke of Peter was when he made an assumption and his question/concern became a demand. On the other hand, Christ did not ignore the questions. Even when the questions were confused, He would explain what they did not understand.

When someone questioning a leader is rebuked, the leader is putting themselves as being just as unquestionable as God's decisions— if not more unquestionable. This means you either worship or fear them more than God. Even as I write this, I constantly question myself, because I do not have complete trust in my own knowledge and reasoning. However, with everything I've found by Scripture and prayer while investigating HH, I cannot let it go to the point of questioning His

Word. This will silence me from questioning my own questions.

Always remember where you are putting your faith.

Getting past the leadership, we have the problem of too many who join HH and some other cults: having their faith in the general community of that cult.

With them pulling in almost all of their members by having them visit and experience the community, this is where one's guard would need to be highest to reach those of this cult.

There is one thing I have heard more than anything else since all of this started. People will constantly say something like, "I still can't believe they would become a part of something like this." It is the difficulty in believing this that can cause the worst presumptions and weak points for the lies to get in.

Hearing a lie, it won't be as hard to doubt as it will be if it comes from someone you love. The lie itself is rarely what convinces you. It is how it is told and who tells it. This is why you must "experience" it. So, beware. If someone convinces you to visit a place like this, you need to remember to make it about finding out what they do and teach and if it is true. It is not to find out about the people there.

It is often sad how the most devoted, strongest, and wisest believers can be those who live in a place of strong persecution. There are many stories about the Christians meeting secretly in China and other countries and how much more devoted they are. This certainly does not mean I should go to China and trust their laws and teaching and promote their structure. It is not something good about the country, it is something about the persecution that strengthens the believers.

When you see a community of loving and devoted people, that does not tell you for certain that they are in a social structure that is teaching Biblically. It only shows you characteristics of the people inside the community. The focus of what we are looking at needs to remain on what they teach and believe, until we know they are following what the Bible teaches and are not giving themselves more authority than is truly theirs.

It is keeping that focus even when you are not going to the point of visiting that is crucial. I don't know how well I would have stood my ground if I was not constantly looking at their teachings to find where they would show me that I was wrong about what they taught or show me the passages that truly showed they were right.

Until they answer the questions, my friends' pleas come from those who are deceived.

This leads to the most challenging part—rejecting the love of those loved ones who joined the cult.

I am consistently hearing stories of others who have lost all communication with friends or family who joined a cult. I heard from some friends who went to HH, but it has been a while now since the last time I got to talk to one of them. And this is a weapon of the cults that can stab deepest into one's heart.

One thing they have done constantly in their comments on my videos is similar to shifting the blame. However, in that case it is more like "shifting the error" than other cases. Yet, it is something they will use all the time, and the place where it can be most effective is when it involves family and friends.

When they demand for members to stop communicating with certain friends or family, one thing they will do is try to make the guilt land on those they are cutting ties with. It is how the one outside the cult is the individual who broke the rule. Thus, it is their fault. The poor logic of these accusations is easy to see. However, just as with the "experience", it is harder to see the logic clearly when hearing this indirectly from one you love. It was hearing friends over the phone accusing me of showing hate and judgment that was harder for me to think clearly about than it was when I got a comment on a video accusing me of the same thing.

I have had to constantly remind myself I am doing it for them, not against them. I am doing it against the deception, not against the deceived. It is crucial to remember they have given themselves up. When they come after you like this, it is not what they think. It is what they are being told they think. Look at it as though it was from someone you did not know so that you can look at it reasonably and not be indoctrinated by who appears to be saying it.

Even if you can have your guard up strong enough to know they are incorrect and what you are saying and doing is correct, there will always be the temptation trying to get in by nothing but how you miss them and don't want to lose them. Again, remember this will not bring them back. It is not by going to what they have become that will get you back in contact with them. Until they have returned to who they truly were and are, you cannot reunite with them. It can be hard to accept this, but it is something you will see evidence of. Do not let that evidence go by unnoticed or wave it off because it did not seem like much.

Having little experience in abuse, I cannot say how closely they compare, but I do see one similarity sticking out to me while watching the deception of these communities and how families are used as a weapon. I have heard of many people abused by their spouse who continually want to keep the relationship going because they know their spouse loves them—even though this may not be true. It is an illusion they put themselves in out of a sort of denial and being too familiar with it. This is what can happen when you have someone you care about trapped in a cult. You keep telling yourself they still love you by ignoring the changes and lies that come in, but you are really talking to someone other than whom you are assuming.

This is where the cult can try to get to you on a far more personal level from multiple angles at once. They use it because it can be the most trying to fight through.

Having yourself prepared for these battles and ready to question, as much as necessary, is not going to make the fight easy. You may have what you need, but it will always be trying.

Of all the things driving me to write this and warn people, the one that pushes me hardest is the concern from how unprepared my friends and I were for something like this to happen. Many felt like they were growing in every sense, and I worry it was overconfidence from this that weakened their guard enough for something to get in.

Sitting back and watching Zach with my mouth shut, I was overconfident in our strength as well.

This is why I need to warn as much as possible. Anything leading away from Christ is the most dangerous kind of threat we can face. Cults are the ones where people (Christians in particular) are the least guarded. It is a place where Satan is not trying to convince us he does not exist. Instead, he is trying to convince us he always exists somewhere we would not go.

There are many times I've heard warnings of how the Mormon church and the JW's try to make themselves look as Christian as possible. However, until HH came along, I never heard about how some cults could do the same thing so much more effectively. I was given the impression it would always be obvious how weird of a religion a cult followed.

Is a cult going to get through and trick you if you stay on guard? No. But staying on guard requires something being used and held in the right place that I believe even Scripture shows us we need to keep a hold of more than most—faith.

***

While going through all of the words HH uses incorrectly, the one that I said frustrated me most is "faith". The reason is more than just how it messes with the gospel in such blunt ways. It is also how their definition hinders its use.

> In all circumstances take up the shield of faith, with which you can extinguish all the flaming darts of the evil one; and take the helmet of salvation, and the sword of the spirit which is the word of God, praying at all times in the Spirit, with all prayer and supplication.
> -   Ephesians 6:16-18 (ESV)

Here you have four tools it speaks of, and two it specifically pushes—faith, salvation, the Word of God, and prayer. Each of these I've shown how HH wants to keep you from holding onto them or make you hold a false form of them.

Salvation they take from you by giving you a conditional form of love. They want to be able to take that helmet from you whenever they choose. The Word of God they will only give you portions of to use and, thereby, limit what you are able to use it against.

But there are two Paul not only says are important but also necessary for us to choose to take in *all* circumstances and at *all* times. Prayer and faith are musts cults completely flip. Prayer in HH is all about you making enough noise you can't hear Him, instead of calling to Him to follow His response. Faith is made to be about your faithfulness in what you do, not your trust in what He does.

Faith in Him… fully in Him… not in others… not in teachings… not in any rules… not in leaders… not in communities… not even in our selves. It has to be in Him. If that is where all of our faith is placed, our guard will be up. Just as Satan did with Eve, they will try to make us look at what God said differently. They want us to listen more to how they want to say things are than what God said they were.

Faith in Him is what keeps us shielded. It is that guard that needs to be kept up. I always found it interesting how the two pieces of the armor that are actually tools and not just something worn are faith and both Scripture and prayer. If we hold on to our faith, and it is led by His Word and prayer, everything else is there in place as our armor.

These cults are all about finding faith in their community and leader(s). It says we are "saved through faith" and "not a result of works". (Eph. 2:8-9 ESV) Everything needs to be about faith in Him. Not faith in our own faithfulness, nor the faithfulness of others.

If we have that guard up, it is simple. The part that makes it difficult is how that shield needs to be held up in ALL circumstances. We (and yes, myself) have constantly lowered our shields or pointed them in the wrong direction too often while in certain situations.

Prayer is going to be happening constantly if faith is being held the right way. What I often remind people of, because I know I need to keep reminding myself of it, is that prayer is not only about speaking to Him but also listening to Him.

When lies are coming our way, we need to be listening to Him the whole time to be sure our faith is in Christ, not in those teaching about Him. If we can continue calling to Him, and listening to Him, we will not have that hole we will be unknowingly led to fill with trust in someone who may become a false god or tool of Satan.

Prayer is also required, because all our union with other parts of the body of Christ is due to our union with and reliance on Him. If we have our union in anything else, even what may seem as good a thing to unite in as our beliefs and teachings, our faith is in the wrong place.

It is when discussions in a Bible study are not always in complete agreement and it does not affect the relationships of those in them that I feel most at ease. It shows me we truly care about one another. We care enough to let them know when things may be different, and we also care enough we won't let small disagreements get in the way of a friendship.

In cults, that is not allowed.

In HH, if you disagree, you must not be a part of the Body anymore and need to go through communion to be reunited with them. Keep your faith where it should be, and you won't be able to be a part of a cult. Just be sure it is, at all times, in Him and listening to Him.

Once again, may we listen to I Cor. and put love first. This is a war, but not because of a desire to cause pain. It is a war to stop those causing the pain. It is a war to protect those being deceived and taken advantage of.

There are many gifts we are to use in this war. God has many different parts for each of us to play in this. Paul tells we need to follow what he gives us to do, but he also says there are three things that are the most helpful for all who are trying to grow in Christ—faith, hope, and love.

I just discussed what makes faith so crucial in this battle. The second part is hope. Hope is necessary because of how little we are able to do, and how we do not know the future and His plan the way God does. As discussed, the best thing we can do is show them our care for them and pray their eyes are opened. It is the waiting and inability to push that makes hope so crucial.

It is why prayer is the other thing we need to have at all times. Prayer is how we are putting our hope in Him. We are giving it to Him and letting Him handle it. It is the consistency of it that keeps our hopes from draining. It is hope in Him that has no end to its power and use. Hope in anything else will weaken and that thing may fail. If Jesus is our hope, we will always have it.

If we keep this hope in place, we will be in prayer, thus, always listening to Him. When the time comes for something to be done, this keeps us ready to act.

But love is the greatest of the three, because it is important not just in and of itself, but also in both faith and prayer. It is the calling upon Him and seeking His will that shows our love for Him and those we seek to bring back. It is our faith in Him that has more meaning than we may realize.

I John 4:8 says "God is love." Faith in Him means we have faith in love. Without His love, there is none. When we have this shield of faith, it is not just about our love for Him and our love for our friends and family. It is also about His love for all of us. That is a power that goes beyond anything we can imagine.

It is the false love people think they find in these communities that pulls them in. It is the love of the people there that they are holding onto so tightly. It is the "love" they are made to believe is the motive of the leaders for their teachings, rules, discipline, and demands.

By holding onto Him and *His* love, we are holding onto love itself. This keeps us in a form of love that is not conditional. It is one that is not flawed and limited. It is what will keep us where we should be to always be ready to take Jesus's example to us by taking those we lost back into our arms when the time comes.

Considering those four things the Bible itself puts as among the most important tools and spiritual gifts to use constantly, we can see more of why Satan uses these cults the way he does.

Faith will be placed in someone, or some people, other than God. Our love will be centered around a community instead of Him. Our prayers will be meant to be heard by other people. And our hope will be in the cult itself or taken away by the fear they will drive inside our hearts. This is how they would be taking from us everything they can of those tools that help us remain strong in Him.

I pray more will keep their guard up. May all find hope to push forward no matter what tricks the enemy pulls. May more hold tight their shields and swords while calling to God for the strength necessary. May more see what love is truly coming from Him. Because I have seen

Satan continuing to pull both us and this world further in the direction of where he will try one more time to take the throne that is not his. That final throne never will be Satan's. May no more try claiming to have it.

Bibliography:

Adams Asahel. "What Is the Gospel?" Homestead Heritage, Dec. 2021, blog.homesteadheritage.com/what-is-the-gospel.

Adams, Blair. *Coming into Orbit: Finding Our Place Within God's Living Order.* Colloquium Press, 2017.

Adams, Blair. *Confession for Baptism and Communion.* Colloquium Press, 2001.

Adams, Blair. *False Faith versus Saving Faith.* Colloquium Press, 2005.

Adams, Blair. *Is the Church Christ On Earth?* Colloquium Press, 2006.

Adams, Blair. *Knowing God by Name: The Creation of a Community That Sustains Life by the Unfolding Self-Revelation of God Through His Name* Colloquium Press, 2010.

Adams, Blair. *Life Against Death: The Struggle for Sustainable Communities From Gandhi to Today.* Colloquium Press, 2008.

Adams, Blair. *Only Two Choices: Two Powers, Two Kingdoms, Two Worlds.* Colloquium Press, 2004.

Adams, Blair. *Questions Visitors Ask.* 1996.

Hassan, Steven. *Freedom of Mind: Helping Loved Ones Leave Controlling People, Cults and Beliefs.* Freedom of Mind Press, 2013.

Welch, Bryan. "Homestead Heritage: Self-Sufficient Living in Action." Mother Earth News, 13 May 2013, www.motherearthnews.com/sustainable-living/nature-and-environment/homestead-heritage-zm0z13jjzcom.